DOES CAPITALISM
HAVE A FUTURE?

DOES CAPITALISM HAVE A FUTURE?

By

IMMANUEL WALLERSTEIN
RANDALL COLLINS
MICHAEL MANN
GEORGI DERLUGUIAN

And

CRAIG CALHOUN

OXFORD
UNIVERSITY PRESS

Oxford University Press is a department of the University of Oxford.
It furthers the University's objective of excellence in research, scholarship,
and education by publishing worldwide.

Oxford New York
Auckland Cape Town Dar es Salaam Hong Kong Karachi
Kuala Lumpur Madrid Melbourne Mexico City Nairobi
New Delhi Shanghai Taipei Toronto

With offices in
Argentina Austria Brazil Chile Czech Republic France Greece
Guatemala Hungary Italy Japan Poland Portugal Singapore
South Korea Switzerland Thailand Turkey Ukraine Vietnam

Oxford is a registered trade mark of Oxford University Press
in the UK and certain other countries.

Published in the United States of America by
Oxford University Press
198 Madison Avenue, New York, NY 10016

© Oxford University Press 2013

Library of Congress Cataloging-in-Publication Data
Wallerstein, Immanuel Maurice, 1930–
   Does capitalism have a future? / By Immanuel Wallerstein, Randall Collins, Michael Mann,
Georgi Derluguian and Craig Calhoun.
      p.   cm.
   ISBN 978–0–19–933084–3 (hardback) — ISBN 978–0–19–933085–0 (paperback) 1. Capitalism.
2. Middle class. 3. Technological innovations—Forecasting. I. Wallerstein, Immanuel. II. Title.
   HB501.W2935 2013
   330.12'2—dc23
                              2013018969
9780199330843
9780199330850 (pbk.)

9 8 7 6 5 4 3 2 1
Printed in the United States of America on acid-free paper

CONTENTS

★

THE NEXT BIG TURN

Collective Introduction

Immanuel Wallerstein, Randall Collins, Michael Mann,
Georgi Derluguian, and Craig Calhoun

Coming decades will deliver surprising shocks and huge challenges. Some of them will look new and some quite old. Many will bring unprecedented political dilemmas and difficult choices. This may well begin to happen soon and will certainly shape the adult lives of those who are young at present. But that, we contend, is not necessarily or only bad. Opportunities to do things differently from past generations will also be arising in the decades ahead. In this book we explore and debate, on the basis of our sociological knowledge of world history, what those challenges and opportunities will most likely be. At bottom, most troubling is that with the end of the Cold War almost three decades ago it has become unfashionable—even embarrassing—to discuss possible world futures and especially the prospects of capitalism.

Our quintet gathered to write this unusual book because something big looms on the horizon: a structural crisis much bigger than the recent Great Recession, which might in retrospect seem only a prologue to a period of deeper troubles and transformations. Immanuel Wallerstein explains the rationale for predicting the breakdown of the capitalist system. Over the next three or four decades capitalists of the world, overcrowding the global markets and hard pressed on all sides by the social and ecological costs of doing business, may find it simply impossible to make their usual investment decisions. In the last five centuries capitalism has been the cosmopolitan and explicitly hierarchical world-market economy where the elite operators, favorably located at its geographical core, were in a position to reap large and reasonably secure profits. But, Wallerstein argues, this historical situation, however dynamic, will ultimately reach its systemic limitations, as do all historical systems. In this hypothesis, capitalism would end in the frustration of capitalists themselves.

Randall Collins focuses on a more specific mechanism challenging the future of capitalism: the political and social repercussions of as many as two-thirds of the educated middle classes, both in the West and globally, becoming structurally unemployed because their jobs are displaced by new information technology. Economic commentators recently discovered the downsizing of the middle class, but they tend to leave the matter with a vague call for policy solutions. Collins systematically considers the five escapes that in the past have saved capitalism from the social costs of its drive for technological innovation. None of the known escapes appears strong enough to compensate for the technological displacement of service and administrative jobs. Nineteenth- and twentieth- century capitalism mechanized manual labor but compensated with the growth of middle- class positions. Now the twenty-first century trajectory of high-tech is to push the middle class into redundancy. This leads us to another hypothesis: Might capitalism end because it loses its political and social cushion of the middle class?

Craig Calhoun argues to the contrary that a reformed capitalism might be saved. Calhoun elaborates on the point, recognized by all of us, that capitalism is not merely a market economy, but a *political* economy. Its institutional framework is shaped by political choice. Structural contradictions may be inherent in the operation of complex markets but it is in the realms of politics that they may be remedied, or left to go unchecked to destruction. Put differently, either a sufficiently enlightened faction of capitalists will face their systemic costs and responsibilities, or they will continue to behave as careless free riders, which they have been able to do since the waning of liberal/left challenges a generation ago. Just how radical will be the shift from contemporary capitalism to a revamped future system is an open question. A centralized socialist economy is one possibility, but Chinese-style state capitalism may be even more likely. Markets can exist in the future even while specifically capitalist modes of property and finance have declined. Capitalism may survive but lose some of its ability to drive global economic integration.

Michael Mann favors a social democratic solution for the problems of capitalism, but he also highlights even deeper problems that arise from the multicausal sources of power. Besides capitalism, these include politics, military geopolitics, ideology, and the multiplicity of world regions. Such complexity, in Mann's view, renders the future of capitalism unpredictable. The overriding threat, which *is* entirely predictable, is the ecological crisis that will grow throughout the twenty-first century. This could likely spill over into struggles over water and food, and result in pollution and massive population migrations, thus raising the prospect of totalitarian reactions and even warfare using nuclear weapons. Mann connects this to the central concern of this book: the future of capitalism. In Mann's analysis, the crisis of climate change is so hard to stop because it derives from all of today's dominant institutions gone global—capitalism as unbridled pursuit of profit, autonomous nation-states insisting on their sovereignty, and individual consumer rights legitimating both modern states and markets. Solving the ecological crisis thus will have to involve a major change in the institutional conditions of today's life.

All these are structural projections akin to "stress tests" in civil engineering or, as we have all now heard, in banking. None of us bases our prognoses of capitalism in terms of condemnation or praise. We have our own moral and political convictions. But as historical sociologists, we recognize that the fortunes of human societies, at least in the last ten thousand years beyond the elementary level of hunter-gatherer bands, have not turned on how much good or evil they produced. Our debate is not whether capitalism is better or worse than any hitherto existing society. The question is: Does it have a future?

This question echoes an old prediction. The expectation of capitalism's collapse was central to the official ideology of the Soviet Union that itself collapsed. Yet does this fact ensure the prospects of capitalism? Georgi Derluguian shows the actual place of the Soviet experiment in the larger picture of world geopolitics, which in the end caused its self-destruction. He also explains how China avoided the collapse of communism while becoming the latest miracle of capitalist growth. Communism was not a viable alternative to capitalism. Yet the way in which the Soviet bloc suddenly ended after 1989 in broad mobilizations from below and blinding panic among the elites may suggest something important about the political future of capitalism.

Doomsday scenarios are not what this book is about. Unlike business and security experts projecting short-run futures by changing the variables in existing set-ups, we consider specific scenarios futile. Events are too contingent and unpredictable because they turn on multiple human wills and shifting circumstances. Only the deeper structural dynamics are roughly calculable. Two of us, the same Collins and Wallerstein who now see no escape for capitalism, already in the 1970s predicted the end of Soviet communism. But nobody could predict either the date or the fact that it would be the former members of the Central Committee irrationally tearing apart their erstwhile industrial and superpower positions. This outcome was unpredictable because it did not have to happen that way.

We find hope against doom exactly in the degree to which our future is politically underdetermined. Systemic crisis loosens and shatters the structural constraints that are themselves the inheritance of past dilemmas and the institutional decisions of prior generations. Business as usual becomes untenable and divergent pathways emerge at such historical junctures. Capitalism, along with its creative destruction of older technologies and forms of production, has also been a source of inequality and environmental degradation. Deep capitalist crisis may be an opportunity to reorganize the planetary affairs of humanity in a way that promotes more social justice and a more livable planet.

Our big contention is that historical systems can have more or less destructive ways of going extinct while morphing into something else. The history of human societies has passed through bursts of revolution, moments of expansive development, and painfully long periods of stagnation or even involution. However unwanted by anybody, the latter remains among the possible outcomes of global crisis in the future. The political and economic structures of present-day capitalism could simply lose their dynamism in the face of rising costs and social pressures. Structurally, this could lead to the world's fragmentation into defensive, internally oppressive, and xenophobic blocs. Some might see it as the clash of civilizations, others as the realization of an Orwellian "1984" anti-utopia enforced by the newest technologies of electronic surveillance. Ways of reestablishing social order in the midst of extreme conflict might include those reminiscent of fascism, but also the possibility of a much broader democracy. It is what we wanted to stress above all in this book.

In recent decades the prevalent opinion in politics and mainstream social sciences has been that no major structural change is even worth thinking about. Neoclassical economics bases its models on the assumption of a fundamentally unchanging social universe. When crises happen, policy adjustments and technological innovation always bring renewals of capitalism. This is, however, only an empirical generalization. Capitalism's existence as a system for 500 years does not prove that it will last forever. The cultural-philosophical critics of various postmodernist persuasions who emerged as a countermovement in the 1980s—when the utopian hopes of 1968 had receded into frustration and Soviet communism was visibly in crisis—came to share the same assumption of capitalism's permanence, although not without a big dose of existential despair. Consequently, the cultural postmodernists left themselves with a dislocation of the will to look structural realities in the face. We will return in our concluding chapter to a more detailed discussion of the present world situation, including its intellectual climate.

We have deliberately written this book in a more accessible style because we intended to open our arguments to wider discussion. The elaboration of our arguments, with all the footnotes, can be found in the monographs that we have written individually. The area where we have done much of our professional research is usually called world-systems analysis or macrohistorical sociology. Macrohistorical sociologists study the origins of capitalism and modern society, as well as the dynamics of ancient empires and civilizations. Seeing social patterns in the longer run, they find that human history moves through multiple contradictions and conflicts, crystallizing over long periods in impermanent configurations of intersecting structures. This is where we had sufficient agreement to author collectively the first and the last chapters bracketing this book. But we also have our particular theories and areas of expertise, and the resulting opinions are reflected in the individual chapters. This short book is not a manifesto sung in one voice. It is a debate of equals arguing on the basis of our knowledge about the past and present of human societies. It is therefore an invitation to ask seriously and openly what could be the next big turn in world history.

In the end, are we prophesying some kind of socialism? The reasoned answer, rather than a futile polemic deriving from ideological faith, must have two parts. First, it is not prophecy because we insist on abiding by the rules of scientific analysis. Here this means showing with reasonable exactness why things may change and how we get from one historical situation to another. Will the end destination be socialism? Our lines of reasoning extend into the middle-range future of the next several decades. Randall Collins asks: what could possibly avert the looming destitution of middle classes whose roles in for-profit market organization become technologically redundant? It could take the form of a socialist reorganization of production and distribution—that is, a political economy in a conscious and collectively coordinated manner designed to make the majority of people relevant. It is thus the structural extension of the problems of advanced capitalism that render socialism the most likely candidate for replacing capitalism. But the lessons of 20th century experience with communist and social democratic states are not forgotten. Socialism had its own problems, mainly from an organizational hypercentralization that provided ample opportunities for political despotism, and the loss of economic dynamism over time. Even if the crisis of capitalism is solved along socialist lines, the problems of socialism will come back into the center of attention. Venturing even further into the long-term future, Collins suggests that socialism itself will not last forever, and the world will oscillate between various forms of capitalism and socialism as each founders on its own shortcomings.

In differently optimistic projections, Craig Calhoun and Michael Mann see the possibility of an alliance of national states uniting in the face of ecological and nuclear disasters. This, they argue, can ensure the continued vitality of capitalism in a more benign social democratic version of globalization. Whatever might come after capitalism, Georgi Derluguian argues that it would never resemble the communist pattern. Fortunately, the historical conditions for the Soviet-style "fortress socialism" are gone, along with the geopolitical and ideological confrontations of the last century. Immanuel Wallerstein, however, considers it intrinsically impossible to tell what might be replacing capitalism. The alternatives are either a noncapitalist system that would nonetheless continue the hierarchical and polarizing features of capitalism, or a relatively democratic and a relatively egalitarian system. Possibly several world-systems will emerge from the transition. Calhoun also argues that more loosely coupled systems may develop to deal with disruptions from external threats as well as the internal risks of capitalism. This runs against the widely shared assumption that the world has become irreversibly global. Yet, once again, what theory supports this ideological contention?

The twentieth century thinkers and political leaders of all persuasions proved to be wrong in their ideological conviction that there was a single road to the future, as passionate advocates of capitalism, communism, and fascism argued and attempted to impose. None of us subscribes to the utopian view that human will can make anything possible. Yet it is demonstrable that our societies can be put together in a certain variety of ways. The result significantly depends on the political visions and wills that prevail in the wake of major crises that produce history's founding moments. Such moments in the past often meant political collapses and revolutions. All five of us, however, strongly doubt that the past revolutions occurring within separate states and often with considerable violence anticipate the future politics of capitalist crisis at the global level. This realization gives us hope that things can be done better in the future.

Capitalism is not a physical location like royal palace or financial district to be seized by a revolutionary crowd or confronted through an idealistic demonstration. Nor is it merely a set of "sound" policies to be adopted and corrected, as prescribed in the business editorials. It is an old ideological illusion of many liberals and Marxists that capitalism simply equals wage labor in a market economy. Such was the basic belief of the twentieth century, on all sides. We are now dealing with its damaging consequences. Markets and wage labor had existed long before capitalism, and social coordination through markets will almost surely outlive capitalism. Capitalism, we contend, is only a particular historical configuration of markets and state structures where private economic gain by almost any means is the paramount goal and measure of success. A different and more satisfying organization of markets and human society may yet become possible.

Grounds for this claim are in this book and our many prior writings. But for the moment, let us offer a short historical fable. Humans have dreamt about flying since ancient times, at least as long as they dreamt about social justice. For several millennia this was fantasy. Then arrived the age of hot air balloons and dirigibles. For about a century people experimented with these devices. The results, as we know, were mixed or downright disastrous. But now there existed engineers, scientists, and the social structure which supported and stimulated their inventiveness. The breakthrough eventually arrived with new kinds of engines and aluminum wings. We can all fly now. The majority are usually stuck in the cramped budget seats, while only the daring can experience the exhilaration of autonomous flight piloting small airplanes or paragliders. Human flight also brought the horrors of aerial bombardment and hovering drones. Technology proposes but humans dispose. Old dreams may come true although this can also impose on us difficult new choices. Yet optimism is a necessary historical condition for mobilizing emotional energies in a world facing the choice of structurally divergent opportunities. Breakthroughs become possible when enough support and public attention go into thinking and arguing about alternative designs.

1

STRUCTURAL CRISIS, OR WHY CAPITALISTS MAY NO LONGER FIND CAPITALISM REWARDING

Immanuel Wallerstein

My analysis is based on two premises: The first is that capitalism is a system, and that all systems have lives; they are never eternal. The second is that to say that capitalism is a system is to say that it has operated by a specific set of rules during what I believe to be its approximately 500 years of existence, and I shall try to state these rules briefly.

Systems have lives. Ilya Prigogine expressed this succinctly: "We have an age, our civilization has an age, our universe has an age. . . . "[1] This means, it seems to me, that all systems from the infinitesimally small to the largest that we know (the universe), including the mid-size historical social systems, should be analyzed as consisting of three qualitatively different

---

[1] Prigogine, *The End of Certainty: Time, Chaos, and the New Laws of Nature* (New York: Free Press, 1996), 166.

moments: the moment of coming into existence; their functioning during their "normal" life (the longest moment); the moment of going out of existence (the structural crisis). In this analysis of the existing situation of the modern world-system, the explanation of its coming into existence is not our subject. But the two other moments of life—the rules of capitalism's functioning during "normal" life, and the modality of its going out of existence—are the central issues before us.

What we are arguing is that, once we have understood what the rules have been that have allowed the modern world-system to operate as a capitalist system, we will understand why it is currently in the terminal stage of structural crisis. We can then suggest how this terminal stage has been operating and is likely to continue to operate for the next 20–40 years.

What are the identifying characteristics, the *sine qua non*, of capitalism as a system, the modern world-system? Many analysts focus on a single institution that they consider crucial: There is wage labor. Or there is production for exchange and/or for profit. Or there is a class struggle between entrepreneurs/capitalists/bourgeoisie and wage-workers/propertyless proletarians. Or there is a "free" market. None of these definitions of defining characteristics holds much water in my opinion.

The reasons are simple. There has been some wage labor across the world for thousands of years, not only in the modern world. Furthermore, there exists much labor that is not wage labor in the modern world-system. There has been some production for profit across the world for thousands of years. But it has never before been the dominant reality of some historical system. The "free market" is indeed a mantra of the modern world-system, but the markets in the modern world-system have never been free of government regulation or political considerations, nor could they have been. There is indeed a class struggle in the modern world-system, but the bourgeois-proletarian description of the contending classes is far too narrowly framed.

In my view, for a historical system to be considered a capitalist system, the dominant or deciding characteristic must be the persistent search for the *endless* accumulation of capital—the accumulation of capital in order to accumulate more capital. And for this characteristic to prevail, there must be mechanisms that penalize any actors who seek to operate on the basis of other values or other objectives, such that these nonconforming actors are sooner or later eliminated from the scene, or at least severely hampered in their ability to accumulate significant amounts of capital. All the many institutions of the modern world-system operate to promote, or at least are constrained by the pressure to promote, the endless accumulation of capital.

The priority of accumulating capital in order to accumulate still more capital seems to me a thoroughly irrational objective. To say that it is irrational, in my appreciation of material or substantive rationality (Weber's *materielle Rationalität*), is not to say that it cannot work in the sense of being able to sustain a historical system, at least for a considerable length of time (Weber's formal rationality). The modern world-system has lasted some 500 years, and in terms of its guiding principle of the endless accumulation of capital it has been extremely successful. However, as we shall argue, the period of its ability to continue to operate on this basis has now come to an end.

Capitalism during Its Phase of "Normal" Operation

How has capitalism worked in practice? All systems fluctuate. That is, the machinery of the system constantly deviates from its point of equilibrium. The example of this with which most people are very familiar is the physiology of the human body. We breathe in and then out. We need to breathe in and out. But there are mechanisms within the human body, and within the modern world-system, to bring the operation of the system back to equilibrium, a moving equilibrium to be sure, but an equilibrium. What we think of as the moment of the "normal" operation of a system is the period during which the pressure to return to equilibrium is greater than any pressure to move away from equilibrium.

There are many such mechanisms in the modern world-system. The two most important—most important in the sense that they are most determinant of the historical development of the system—are what I shall call Kondratieff cycles and hegemonic cycles. Here is how each operates.

First, the Kondratieff cycles: In order to accumulate significant amounts of capital, producers require a quasi-monopoly. Only if they have a quasi-monopoly can they sell their products at prices far above the costs of production. In truly competitive systems with a fully free flow of the factors of production, any intelligent buyer can find sellers who will sell the products for the profit of a penny, or even below the cost of production. There can be no real profit in a perfectly competitive system. Real profit requires limits on the free market, that is, a quasi-monopoly.

However, quasi-monopolies can only be established under two conditions: (1) The product is an innovation for which there exists (or can be induced to exist) a reasonably large number of willing buyers; and (2) One or more powerful states are willing to use state power to prevent (or at least limit) the entry of other producers into the market. In short, quasi-monopolies can only exist if the market is not "free" from state involvement.

We have come to call such quasi-monopolized products "leading products." They are "leading" in the sense that they determine a large percentage of the world-system's economic activity—in their own right, and via their forward and backward linkages. Whenever such quasi-monopolies are established, there follows an expansion of "growth" throughout the world-economy, and the times are perceived overall as times of "prosperity." Such periods are generally periods of high levels of global employment because of the personnel needs of the producers of both the quasi-monopoly and their forward and backward linkages and because of the consumption expenditures of the employed personnel. And while some parts of the world-system and some groups within it no doubt do better than others, for most persons and groups this period of overall growth in production is a situation in which a "rising tide lifts all boats."

The state can do many things to create and preserve such a quasi-monopoly. It can enact it legally, via a system of patents, or other forms of protecting so-called intellectual property. It can offer direct assistance to the quasi-monopolized industry, especially in research and development. It can be a major purchaser, often at inflated prices. It can use its geopolitical strength to try to prevent infringements of such quasi-monopolies by putative producers in other countries.

The advantages of a quasi-monopoly do not last forever. The systemic problem for the producers is that such quasi-monopolies are self-liquidating over time. Again the reason is simple. If such quasi-monopolies are so profitable, obviously other producers will try very hard to enter the market to share in the benefits. There are many ways to do this. If the basis of the quasi-monopoly is some new technology that is being kept secret, they can try either to steal the secret or to duplicate it. If they are being kept out of the market by the geopolitical strength of the country by which the quasi-monopoly is being protected, they can try to marshal alternative geopolitical strength to counter this. They can mobilize anti-monopolistic sentiments inside the enforcing country.

In addition, if one controls a quasi-monopoly, the most immediate concern is to avoid work stoppages, since this involves a major loss of capital,

irrecoverable if the other producers in an oligopoly do not suffer simultaneously from work stoppages. This gives workers a major weapon in their
never-ending search for better conditions. In such situations, the producers consequently often find that concessions to workers cost them less than
work stoppages. Over time, however, this means a creeping increase in the
costs of labor, which reduces the overall margin of profit.

One way or another, other potential producers can wear down the ability
of the producers of the leading products to maintain the quasi-monopoly.
Up to now, it seems to have taken an average of 25–30 years to do this. But,
whatever the length of protection for the leading industry, sooner or later
there comes a point at which the quasi-monopoly is significantly breached.
And this breach brings with it, as predicted by the heralds of capitalism, a
lowering of prices. The lowering of prices may be beneficial to the purchas-
ers but it is of course negative for the sellers. What had been a profitable
leading product has become a more competitive, much less profitable product on the world scene.

What can the producers do? One alternative is to trade the advantage of
low transaction costs for lower production costs. This usually involves the
shifting of primary production locations from one or more "core" locations
to other parts of the world-system where "historic" labor costs are lower.
Persons in these new locations for production may perceive and hail this
entry into the world production nexus as national "development." It is more
properly seen as trickle-down transfer of erstwhile (but no longer) super-
profitable industries.

Relocation of industries is only one kind of response to the changed situation. Producers in erstwhile leading industries can try to maintain some
part of this production in countries where they were historically located by
specializing in a niche subproduct, one that is more difficult to reproduce
quickly elsewhere. They can also negotiate with their workforce to obtain
the lowering of remuneration (in all its multiple forms) by wielding the
threat of still more relocation of industry, and hence still greater unemployment for the workforce in the previous location. In general, the ability of the
working strata to defend their advantages gained in the period of expansion
of the world-economy is severely called into question by this increase in the
competitiveness of the world market.

They can also, in part or in whole, transfer their search for capital from the
production (and even the commercial) sphere, and concentrate on profits

in the financial sector. Today we speak of such "financialization" as though it were an invention of the 1970s. But it is actually a very long-standing practice in all Kondratieff B-phases. As Braudel has shown, the truly successful capitalists have always been those who reject "specialization" in industry, commerce, or finance, preferring to be generalists who move between these processes as opportunities dictate.

lending

How does one make money in the financial sphere? The basic mechanism is to lend money, which has to be repaid with interest. The most rewarding debts to the lenders are those in which the debtor overborrows and therefore can only repay the interest but not the capital. This leads to a recurrent and ever-increasing income to the lender until the debtor is overwhelmed (bankrupt).

Such a financial loan mechanism does not create new real value, not even new capital. It essentially reallocates existing capital. It also requires that there be ever new circles of debtors to replace those who are overwhelmed, in order thereby to maintain the flow of lending and indebtedness. These financial processes can be very profitable to those who are located on the lending side of the equation.

The lending-indebtedness chain does however have one downside from the point of view of the "normal" operation of the capitalist system. It eventually exhausts effective demand for all production. This is both an economic and a political danger to the system, which requires therefore a return to equilibrium, that is, a return to a situation in which capital is accumulated primarily through new production. Schumpeter has shown very clearly how this comes about economically. An invention is transmogrified into an innovation, which results in the emergence of a new leading product that permits the renewed expansion of the world-economy.

The politics of such a transmogrification have been a matter of much debate. It seems to require a strengthening of the position of the working classes in the class struggle. It may require a willingness of some part of the producing classes to accede to this stronger position of the working strata— a sacrifice of short-run individual profits in the interests of the longer-run collective profits of the producing classes.

This pattern of expansion and contraction of capitalism is only possible because capitalism is not a system that is located within a single state, but is rather ensconced in a world-system, larger by definition than any single state. If these processes were occurring in a single state, there would be nothing to prevent the holders of state power from appropriating the surplus value, which would remove (or at least considerably reduce) the incentive of entrepreneurs to develop new products. On the other hand, were there no states whatsoever within the range of the market, there would be no way to obtain quasi-monopolies. It is only if capitalists are located in a "world-economy"—one that has a multiplicity of states within it—that entrepreneurs can pursue the endless accumulation of capital.

This then explains why we have so-called hegemonic cycles, ones that are considerably longer than the Kondratieff cycles. What is meant by hegemony in a world-economy is the ability of one state to impose a set of rules on the operation of all other states, such that there is relative order in the world-system. The importance of "relative" order is something on which Schumpeter insisted in his theorizing. Disorders—interstate and intrastate (civil) wars, mafiosi protection rackets, extensive official and institutional corruption, rampant petty crime—are all profitable to small sectors of the world's population. But they all hinder the global search for maximizing the accumulation of capital. Indeed, they bring about the destruction of much infrastructure necessary for the maintenance and expansion of capitalist accumulation.

It follows that the imposition of relative order by a hegemonic power is a positive benefit for the "normal" operation of the capitalist system as a whole. It is also of great benefit to the hegemonic power itself—its state, its entrepreneurs, its ordinary citizens. There is reason to doubt that the benefits to the system as a whole (and to the hegemonic power) also bring in their wake a benefit to other states and their enterprises and citizens. Therein lays the tension, and the explanation, of why achieving and maintaining hegemony is so difficult and so rare.

The pattern of hegemonic cycles heretofore has been that after a very destructive "thirty years' war" between the two powers that had been in the best position to seek to be the dominant power in the world-system, one of them wins out decisively. At that point, one state combines in its economic processes marked advantage simultaneously in all three forms of economic activity—production, commerce, and finance. Such a state furthermore enjoys, as a result of its strong economic base and its successful victory in the previous struggle, a significant military edge. And to cap its overall position, it asserts cultural dominance, including the defining version of the geoculture (Gramsci's concept of hegemony).

With this combination of preeminence in all spheres of the world-system, it can obtain its objectives and impose its will, most of the way most of the time. We may think of this as a quasi-monopoly of geopolitical power. At the outset, this hegemonic dominance does indeed create relative order in the world-system and relative stability. The problem here, as in the case of the quasi-monopolies of leading industries, is that quasi-monopolies of geopolitical power are self-liquidating, for several reasons.

First, there are always clear losers in a situation of relative stability. They begin to rebel in multiple ways. To contain their rebellions, the hegemonic power finds it necessary to engage in repressive activities, often military activities. Repressive activities may often be, in the immediate sense, quite successful. But the use of force always brings with it two negative consequences. The military action is often less than totally successful, thereby exposing some limitations to the hegemonic power's repressive powers. This thereupon tends to embolden future shows of defiance.

Secondly, the employment of repressive force contains a price for the armies and other institutions of the hegemonic power. The cost in lives (deaths and damaged lives) grows steadily. And the financial costs begin to mount. Slowly but surely, this undermines the popular support for this activity, as the populace begins to perceive more clearly the gains (usually disproportionately to a subset of the hegemonic power's population) and the losses (usually to a much larger subset). As a result, the authorities of a hegemonic power begin to feel internal constraints on their ability to impose world order.

Thirdly, other states, which had fallen far behind the hegemonic power in terms of geopolitical strength at the beginning of the period of hegemonic dominance, begin to recover their strength and begin to insist on a larger geopolitical role. The world-system begins to move away from a situation of undisputed hegemony to a situation of balance of powers. Since the process is cyclical, there begin to be efforts by others to seek the role of successor hegemonic power. But this is a complicated and arduous process, which explains why hegemonic cycles are so much longer than Kondratieff cycles.[2] Because of all this, the hegemonic power begins to experience a slow decline.

---

[2] I explain this process in "The Concept of Hegemony in a World-Economy," in Prologue to the 2011 Edition of *The Modern World-System, II: Mercantilism and the Consolidation of the European World-Economy, 1600–1750* (Berkeley: Univ. of California Press, 2011), xxii–xxvii.

There is one last element to stress in this description of the ongoing processes of the modern world-system. Both Kondratieff cycles and hegemonic cycles are cycles. But they are never perfect cycles, in the sense of returning in the end to the starting point. This is because the A-phases of these two cycles involve growth—in real value, in geographic scope, in depth of commodification. It is never possible in the B-phase to eradicate all this growth. Rather, the return to equilibrium represented by the B-phase is at best a partial regression of the system, what might be better described as a "stagnation" of the system rather than a full regression to the system's previous positions in whatever criteria we measure.

We might diagram this as a ratchet effect, two steps forward and one step backward. Thus the cyclical rhythms of the historical system create a moving equilibrium, which translates into secular trends upward of its principal curves. If we draw this on a plane, with the y-axis or ordinate measuring the percentages of some phenomenon and the x-axis or abscissa measuring time, we have curves that are slowly moving toward asymptotes (100% of what is being measured on the y-axis). As the system approaches these asymptotes, it is thereby moving steadily further from equilibrium, since one can never cross the asymptote. It seems that once these curves reach somewhere about the 80% point, the system starts to oscillate rapidly and repeatedly, becomes "chaotic," and bifurcates. We can say that this is the point at which the system has arrived at the beginning of its structural crisis. We shall now try to offer concrete evidence for how this has been occurring in our historical system.

THE MODERN WORLD-SYSTEM, 1945 TO CIRCA 1970

The last great struggle for hegemony was that between Germany and the United States, a struggle that can be considered to have begun more or less in 1873 and which culminated in a "thirty years' war" that ran from 1914 to 1945. With Germany's "unconditional surrender" in 1945, the United States was the clear and acknowledged victor in this struggle.

The United States emerged from what we refer to as the Second World War endowed with incredible economic strength. Its economic capacity and competitiveness had already been very strong before the war began. The war enlarged this strength in two ways. On the one hand, all the other industrial powers in the world-system—from Great Britain across Europe to the

Union of Soviet Socialist Republics (U.S.S.R.) to Japan—suffered grievous damage to their material plant. In addition, because of wartime destruction of their agricultural production, most of them were also suffering from serious food shortages in the immediate postwar period. In great contrast on the other hand, the United States, sheltered as it had been from physical damage, was able to develop still further its industrial and agricultural base throughout the war. Not only the defeated Axis powers but even the wartime allies of the United States sought immediate relief and reconstruction aid from the United States.

We can measure the degree of initial advantage in a very simple way. In any major sector of production in the first 10–15 years after 1945, the United States was able to sell products in all the other industrialized countries at lower levels of cost (including transport) than the local producers.

The one sphere in which the United States did not have an excessive advantage was the military sphere. The Soviet Union possessed a very strong military force, and its troops were occupying a large segment of territory in east-central Europe and northeast Asia (Manchuria and Inner Mongolia in China, the northern half of Korea, and southern Sakhalin and the Kuril Islands in Japan). It is true that as of 1945 the United States had nuclear weapons, but even this advantage would evaporate by 1949.

As a result, if the United States were going to play the role of hegemonic power, it would have to come to some kind of terms with the Soviet Union and neutralize its military strength. This was particularly true since internal political pressure in the United States led to a relatively rapid demobilization of its land forces worldwide.

It is my contention that what ensued was a tacit "deal" between the United States and the Soviet Union, to which we have given the metaphorical name of Yalta. It seems to me that this deal had three components. The first was a de facto division of the globe into two spheres of influence, more or less along the lines of the location of the armed forces of each of the two countries at the end of the war. There was a Soviet bloc, which would come to be defined as running from the Oder-Neisse line in central Europe to the 38th Parallel in Korea (and including mainland China, after the definitive defeat of the Kuomintang by the Chinese Communist Party forces in 1949).

What the United States and the Soviet Union in effect agreed to observe was the primary (virtually exclusive) right of each to decide matters within its sphere. A crucial element of this de facto agreement was there would be no attempt to change these boundaries by military (or even political) means. After 1949, this accord was reinforced by the concept of "mutually assured destruction" based on the fact that both sides had sufficient nuclear strength to respond to any attack and destroy the other.

The second part of the tacit agreement was the de facto economic disjuncture of the two zones. The United States would offer no assistance in the reconstruction of the Soviet bloc. Its aid would be limited to its zone—the Marshall Plan in western Europe, comparable aid to Japan and later to South Korea and Taiwan in east Asia. US aid to its allies was not simply altruistic philanthropy. It needed customers for its flourishing industries, and reconstructing the economy of these allies made them good customers, as well as faithful political satellites. The Soviet Union in turn developed its own regional economic structures, ones that reinforced the autarkic character of the Soviet zone.

The third part of the "deal" was to deny that there was any deal. Each side proclaimed very loudly in its particular language that it was in a total ideological struggle with the other. We came to call this the "Cold War." Note however that it was and remained to the end a "cold" war. The purpose of the very loud rhetoric was not in reality to transform the other, at least not before some very distant moment when the other side would somehow crumble. In this sense neither side was trying in any immediate time span to "win" the war. Each sought rather to oblige its satellites (euphemistically called allies) to toe a very strict political line, as dictated by the two superpowers. Neither side would ever support in any meaningful sense rebellious forces within the other camp, since this might lead to the undoing of the primary agreement of a military status quo between the two superpowers.

Once the military status quo was achieved, the United States could proceed to realize its overall political and cultural dominance in the world-system—with its automatic majorities in the United Nations and multiple other transnational institutions. The sole exception was in the one agency that controlled military matters—the U.N. Security Council, where the veto power of each side ensured the military status quo.

This arrangement worked very well in the beginning. And then the self-liquidating character of a geopolitical quasi-monopoly began to take its toll. The two most significant geopolitical changes in the two decades following 1945 were revolts in the Third World and the economic recovery of western Europe and Japan.

What were labeled then as Third World countries (and which we tended later to call the South) had very little to gain in the geopolitical status quo that the two superpowers were attempting to impose on the world. Some of them began to defy the arrangements. The Chinese Communist Party refused to make a deal with the Kuomintang, as the Soviet Union wanted them to do. Instead they defeated the Kuomintang and came to state power. The Viet Minh and the Viet Cong proceeded on their own path, defeating both the French and the Americans. Fidel Castro and his guerrillas came to power, and almost upset the world apple cart in 1962. The Algerians went forward to independence to the chagrin (at least initially) of the French Communist Party. And Nasser successfully took control of the Suez Canal.

Neither the United States nor the Soviet Union was in fact happy with this turmoil. Each adjusted to this reality in similar ways. Initially, each side insisted on a forced choice of loyalties in the Cold War, believing, as the then US Secretary of State, John Foster Dulles, famously said, that "there are no neutrals." But later, both sides felt it necessary to soften their stance and try instead to woo those who sought to be neutral. In the process, the Soviet Union "lost" China. And the United States paid a very heavy economic and political price for its Vietnam War.

The other change—one that affected the United States more than the Soviet Union—may be seen in the political consequences of economic recovery in the midst of the incredibly expansive Kondratieff A-phase that prevailed. By the early 1960s, it was no longer true that the United States could sell automobiles (for example) more cheaply in Germany or Japan than local producers. Indeed, the contrary was beginning to occur. German and Japanese automobiles were successfully entering the US market.

The new economic strength of the erstwhile satellites of the United States turned them into genuine competitors on the world market. By the late 1960s, the United States no longer held a significant economic edge over its major allies in the sphere of world production, or even in transnational commerce. The basis of geopolitical hegemony was beginning to fray.

After 1945, the world-system enjoyed the largest (by far) expansion in capital accumulation that it had ever known since the launching of the modern world-system in the long sixteenth century. After 1945, the world-system also enjoyed the largest (by far) expansion of geopolitical power in the period of US hegemony that it had ever known since the launching of the modern world-system. These two cycles were simultaneous and reached the point of self-liquidation more or less simultaneously. The biggest upturns would be followed by the biggest downturns. The world-system had in the process moved very far from equilibrium as an historical system. Its restorative mechanisms seemed to have been stretched beyond repair. It was now entering into structural crisis.

THE STRUCTURAL CRISIS, CIRCA 1970 TO ?

There were two crucial developments that contributed to this structural crisis. The first had to do with the long-term secular trends of the world-economy, which would now make it extremely difficult for capitalists to accumulate capital endlessly. And the second had to do with the conjunctural end of the dominance by centrist liberals of the geoculture, which would undermine the political stability of the world-system. Let me treat each in turn.

Long-Term Structural Trends

How does one accumulate capital endlessly in a capitalist system? The basic method, albeit not the only one, is via production, in which the entrepreneur-producer retains the differential between what it costs to produce the commodity and the price at which the producer can sell it. The lower the costs and the higher the sales price, the more profit is realized and can then be reinvested.

But how can the differential between costs and sales price be maximized? There are two necessary elements in this exercise. To maximize sales price, there must be a quasi-monopoly, a subject we have already treated. It is how one in addition minimizes costs that we must now discuss. We start with the reality that there are always three generic costs in any productive process. These are personnel costs, the costs of inputs, and taxation.

There are three different levels of personnel for whom the producer/owner has to pay: the unskilled and semiskilled workforce, the skilled workers and supervisory cadres, and the top managers. The costs of the least skilled workforce tend to go up in A-phases, as they collectively make demands on the employer in one form or other of syndical action. Employers during A-phases may make concessions to the least skilled personnel because avoiding shutdowns or slowdowns may be less costly than wage increases. However, eventually these costs become too high for the employ-ers, particularly for those in the leading industries.

The solution for employers has historically been the runaway factory, that is, relocation to "historically" lower-wage areas during the B-period. There the workers are recruited from loci (usually rural) in which their real income is even lower than that offered by the newly installed (usually urban) production site. It seems to be a win-win situation for the worker and the employer. After some time, however, the transplanted workers feel more knowledgeable about their new situation and more aware of the low level of their wages in worldwide terms. They begin to engage in some syndical action. And sooner or later the employer finds that, as a result, the costs have again become too high. The solution is still another move.

The moves are costly but effective. Worldwide there is, however, a ratchet effect. The reductions never eliminate totally the increases. Over 500 years, this repeated process has virtually exhausted the loci into which to move. This can be measured by the degree of deruralization of the world-system, which has risen spectacularly in the last fifty years and seems to be proceed-ing apace.

The increase in the costs of cadres is the result of two different consider-ations. One, the constantly increased scale of productive units requires more intermediate personnel to coordinate it. And two, the political dangers that result from the repeated syndical organization of the relatively low-skilled personnel are countered by the creation of a larger intermediate stratum who can be both political allies for the ruling stratum and models of a possi-ble upward mobility for the unskilled majority, thereby blunting its political mobilization. Their salaries significantly increase the overall personnel bill.

The increase in the costs of top managers is the direct result of the in-creased complexity of entrepreneurial structures—the famous separation of ownership and control. This makes it possible for these top managers to appropriate ever larger portions of the firm's receipts as rent, thereby reduc-ing what goes to the "owners" (shareholders) as profit or to the firm for rein-vestment This last increase was quite spectacular in size during the last few decades.

The costs of inputs have been going up for analogous reasons. Capitalists seek to externalize as many costs as they can. This is an elegant way of saying that they are not paying the full bill for the inputs they use. The three main costs they are able to externalize are the disposal of toxic waste, the renewal *extern.*

of raw materials, and the construction of the necessary infrastructure for transport and communications. Over most of the history of the modern world-system, it was considered normal practice to externalize such costs. It was seldom a concern for political authorities.

In the last few decades, however, the political atmosphere has changed radically. Climate change is a very widely debated issue, as a result of which there has been much demand for "green" and "organic" products. The past "normality" of externalization is a distant memory. The explanation for the new political debate about toxic disposal is rather simple. The world has largely run out of vacant public domains into which to dump waste. This is equivalent in effect to that of the deruralization of the world's work force, the running-out of new groups of potential low-wage workers. The impact on public health has become high and obvious. The result has been the growth of social movements making demands for environmental cleanup and control.

Secondly, public concern about the renewal of resources—another new political reality—is in large part the consequence of the sharp increase in world population. Suddenly, the world has discovered asset shortages of many kinds, already existing or soon to be felt: energy sources, water, forests, fish, and meat. There is debate about who owns what, who uses what, for what purposes the resources are used, and who pays the bill.

Thirdly, capitalism as a system requires considerable infrastructure. Products produced for sale on the world market must be transported. Communication is a crucial element in commerce. Transport and communication are today far more efficient and much, much faster. But this has also meant that the costs have risen considerably. Who pays for this? In the past, the producers who have made the most use of the infrastructure have paid only a small part of the bill. The general public has paid the rest.

Today there is strong political demand that governments assume a new direct role in ensuring detoxification, resource renewal, and further infrastructure expansion. This would require that governments increase taxes significantly. In addition, there is no point in doing this if the causes of the negative realities go untouched. This means that governments would need to insist on more internalization of costs by entrepreneurs. Both increased taxes and, even more, requirements for internalization of these costs would cut sharply into the margins of profit of enterprises—a point that is constantly made by the producers.

Finally, taxation in all its forms has been going up over the historical life of the modern world-system. All the multiple political levels of government require taxation, both to pay the personnel and to pay for the expanding services these governments are expected to offer. There is also the expansion of what might be called private taxation—both the corruption of government officials and the predatory demands of organized mafias. Private taxation is a cost to the entrepreneur, just as much as is state taxation. As the size of governmental structures has vastly increased, particularly in the last fifty years, there have been more people to bribe. And as world economic activity has grown, there is ever more room for mafiosi operations.

Still, the biggest source of increased taxation has resulted from the political struggles of the world's antisystemic movements. Their demands over the past two centuries have brought about the democratization of world politics. The program of popular movements has fundamentally been to obtain from the states three basic guarantees for the citizenry—education, health services, and lifelong revenue flows. The demands for each have steadily expanded in two ways over the past 200 years: the levels of services demanded, and therefore the costs; and the geographical locales in which the demands have been made. These expenditures are what we refer to as the "welfare state"—a form of which is now part of the normal political life of virtually every government in the world, even if the level of what is offered varies, in large part according to the wealth level of the country.

We can sum this up by saying that the three basic costs of production have risen constantly and have now each approached close enough to their asymptotes that the system cannot be brought back to equilibrium via the multiple mechanisms that have been used for 500 years. The possibilities for producers to achieve an endless accumulation of capital seem to be ending.

A Major Geocultural Change

The profit squeeze for capitalist producers has been compounded by a colossal cultural change. This is the end of the dominance of centrist liberalism in the geoculture, which is the meaning and the consequence of the world-revolution of 1968. The story of the world-revolution of 1968 is in large part the story of the antisystemic movements in the modern world-system—their birth, their strategy, their history up to 1968, their importance for the political operation of the modern world-system.

During the nineteenth century, the Old Left, as it came to be called during the world-revolution of 1968, consisted essentially of the two varieties of world social movements, the Communists and the Social Democrats, plus the national liberation movements. These movements grew slowly and with great effort, primarily during the last third of the nineteenth century and the first half of the twentieth century. For a long time, they were weak and politically somewhat marginal. And then in the period 1945 to 1968, they became extremely strong rather rapidly, again in almost all parts of the world-system.

It seems somewhat counterintuitive that they should have achieved such strength precisely during the period of both the extraordinary Kondratieff A-phase expansion and the height of US hegemony. I do not think, however, that this was fortuitous. Recall that I argued that capitalists have a strong desire not to experience interruptions of their production processes (strikes, slowdowns, sabotage) when the world-economy is flourishing, especially those capitalists involved in the most profitable processes, the leading industries. Given that the expansion at this time was exceptionally profitable, the producers were ready to make significant wage concessions to their workers, believing that such concessions would cost them less than the profit losses resulting from such interruptions. To be sure, this meant middle-term rising costs of production, which would become a major factor in the decline of the quasi-monopolies in the late 1960s. But most entrepreneurs, then as always, calculated their interests in terms of short-term profits, feeling unable to predict or control what might happen after about three years.

The hegemonic power thought about its interests in somewhat similar ways. Its primary concern was to maintain a relative stability in the geopolitical arena. Repressive activity on the world scene against the antisystemic movements seemed very costly. Where possible—it was not always possible—the United States favored a "decolonization" that was negotiated, resulting in a regime that presumably could be expected to be more "moderate" in its future politics. This had the effect of bringing nationalist/national liberation movements to power in a very large swath of Asia, Africa, and the Caribbean.

In the great internal debates of the movements in the late nineteenth century—Marxists versus anarchists in the social movements in the industrialized countries, political versus cultural nationalism in the anticolonial movements—the Marxists and the political nationalists argued that the only credible program was the so-called two-step strategy: first take state

power, then change the world. By 1945, the Marxists and the political nationalists had clearly gained the upper hand in the intra-movement debates
and controlled the most powerful organizations.[3]

These relatively permissive attitudes of the megacorporations and the hegemonic power had the consequence that, by the middle of the 1960s, the
Old Left movements had achieved their historic goal of state power almost
everywhere. Communist parties were in power in one-third of the world,
called at the time the socialist bloc. Social Democratic parties were in alter-
nating power in most of another third of the world—the pan-European
world.[4] And, by 1968, in almost all of the colonial countries, the nationalist and national liberation movements had come to power.[5]

However "moderate" many of these movements seemed when in power,
the world-system was pervaded at the time by a significant triumphalism that
all these movements affected. They felt and loudly proclaimed that the future
was theirs, that history was on their side. And the powerful in the modern
world-system were afraid these proclamations were accurate. They feared the
worst. However, those who participated in the world-revolution of 1968 did
not agree. They did not see the coming to power of the Old Left movements
as a triumph, but rather as a betrayal. They said in essence: You may be in
power (step one) but you haven't changed the world at all (step two).

---

[3] It is true that the "Marxists" divided into two camps as of the Russian Revolution, the
Social Democrats (or 2nd International) and the Communists (or 3rd International). However, their differences were not about the two-step strategy, but rather about how to achieve
the first step—taking state power. Furthermore, by 1968, the Social Democrats had stopped
calling themselves Marxists, while the Communists were now calling themselves Marxist-
Leninists. For the young persons who made up the bulk of the participants in the world-
revolution of 1968, this debate between the adherents of the two Internationals, so important to the Old Left, seemed almost irrelevant, as these young persons tended to have dispar-
aging opinions about both varieties of Old Left social movements.

[4] One has to remember that, at that time, the principal policy of the Social Democratic
parties—the welfare state—was accepted by their conservative alternate parties, which
merely quibbled about the details. I consider New Deal liberals in the United States to be a
variety of Social Democrats who simply declined to utilize the label for reasons peculiar to
the political history of the United States.

[5] Most Latin American countries had become formally independent in the first half of the
nineteenth century. But populist movements there showed analogous strength to national
liberation movements in the still formally colonial world.

If one listened carefully to the rhetoric of participants in the world-revolution of 1968, and one ignored the local references (which were of course different from one country to another), there were three themes that seemed to pervade the analyses of those who engaged in these multiple uprisings, whether they were located in the socialist bloc, the pan-European world, or the Third World.

The first theme concerned the hegemonic power. The United States was not seen as the guarantor of world order; it was seen as the imperialist overlord, but one that had overstretched and was now vulnerable. The Vietnam War was then at its height, and the Tet offensive of February 1968 was considered to be the death knell of the US military operation. This was not all. The revolutionaries accused the Soviet Union of being a collusive partner in US hegemony.

The Cold War was, they believed, a phony facade. The Yalta deal of de facto status quo was the major geopolitical reality. This deep suspicion had been growing since 1956. 1956 was the year of Suez and Hungary—in which neither superpower acted in terms of Cold War rhetoric. It was also the year of Khrushchev's "secret" talk at the 20th Congress of the Communist Party of the Soviet Union, a talk that undid Stalinist rhetoric and many of his policies, leading to a widespread "disillusionment" among the erstwhile faithful.

The second theme concerned the Old Left movements, which were attacked everywhere for failing to fulfill their promises (the second step) when they came to power. The militants said in effect that, since you haven't changed the world, we must rethink a failed strategy and replace you with new movements. For many, it was the Chinese Cultural Revolution that served as a model—with their call to purge the "capitalist roaders" in the very top positions of the party and government.

The third theme concerned what might be called the forgotten peoples—those oppressed because of their race, their gender, their ethnicity, their sexuality, their otherness in all its possible guises. The Old Left movements had all been hierarchical movements, insisting that only one movement in any country could be "the" revolutionary movement, and that this movement had to give priority to a particular type of struggle—the class struggle in the industrialized countries (the North), the national struggle in the rest of the world (the South).

The logic of their position was that any "group" that sought to pursue an autonomous strategy was undermining the priority struggle and therefore was objectively counter-revolutionary. All such groups had to be organized within the hierarchical party structure and be subordinate to its topdown tactical decisions.

The 1968 militants insisted that the demands for equal treatment by all of these groups could no longer be deferred to some putative future time after the main struggle was "won." These demands were urgent and the oppression they were combating was as important as that of the alleged priority group in the present. The forgotten peoples included prominently women, socially defined minorities (racial, ethnic, religious), persons of multiple sexual tendencies, and persons who gave priority to ecological issues or peace struggles. There is no end to the list of forgotten peoples, which has expanded and become more militant ever since. At the time, the Black Panthers in the United States were a very prominent example of this kind of group.

The world-revolution of 1968 (actually it occurred over a period going from 1966 to 1970) did not lead to a political transformation of the world-system. Indeed, in most countries, the movement was successfully repressed, and many of its participants abandoned their youthful enthusiasms as the years went by. But it did leave a lasting legacy. The ability of centrist liberals to insist that their version of the geoculture was the only legitimate one was destroyed in the process. Exponents of truly conservative and truly radical ideologies resumed their autonomous existence, and began to pursue autonomous organizational and political strategies.

The consequence of this cultural-political change for the operation of the modern world-system was enormous. Having entered into a critical situation in terms of the ability of capitalists to pursue the endless accumulation of capital, the political stability of the modern world-system was no longer guaranteed by the overwhelming strength of centrist liberalism with its assurances of an ever-better future for everyone, provided only one patiently submitted to the wise actions of the persons with the specialized capacity to bring about this ever-better future, eventually.

The Chaos That Ensued

The world-revolution of 1968 was an enormous political success. The world-revolution of 1968 was an enormous political failure. It seemed to spread and flourish across the globe, yet by the mid-1970s seemed to be extinguished almost everywhere. What had been accomplished by this wild brushfire? Actually, quite a bit. Centrist liberalism had been dethroned as the governing ideology of the world-system, the de facto only legitimate ideology. It was now reduced to being simply one alternative among others. In addition, the Old Left movements were destroyed as mobilizers of any kind of fundamental change. Still, the immediate triumphalism of the revolutionaries of 1968, liberated from any subordination to centrist liberalism, proved shallow and unsustainable.

The world right was equally liberated from any attachment to centrist liberalism. It took advantage of the world economic stagnation and the collapse of the Old Left movements (and their governments) to launch a counteroffensive, which we call neoliberal (actually quite conservative) globalization. The prime objectives were to reverse all the gains of the lower strata during the Kondratieff A-period. The world right sought to reduce all the major costs of production, to destroy the welfare state in all its versions, and to slow down the decline of US power in the world-system. The onward march of the world right seemed to culminate in 1989. The ending of Soviet control over its east-central European satellite states, and the dismantling of the Soviet Union itself in 1991, led to a sudden new triumphalism of the world right.

The offensive of the world right was a great success. The offensive of the world right was a great failure. With the onset of the world economic stagnation in the 1970s (the Kondratieff B-phase), large capitalist producers did shift significant amount of productive activity to new zones, which did seem to "develop" significantly. But however beneficial this was to the local middle strata in these countries, whose numbers now expanded considerably, the amount of capital accumulation, seen at a global level, was not all that impressive and did not begin to match what these corporate producers had been able to accumulate during the 1945–1970 period.

To maintain a level of massive appropriation of world surplus value, capitalists had to turn to obtaining it in the financial sector—what has come to be called the "financialization" of the world-system. As suggested previously, such financialization has been a cyclically recurring feature of the modern world-system for 500 years.

What was sustaining the accumulation of capital since the 1970s was the turning from seeking profits via productive efficiency to seeking profits via financial manipulations, more correctly called speculation. The key mechanism of speculation is encouraging consumption via indebtedness. (This is of course what has happened in every Kondratieff B-phase.) What was different this time has been its scale and the ingenuity of the new financial instruments used to pursue speculative activity. The biggest A-phase expansion in the history of the capitalist world-economy has been followed by the biggest speculative mania.

It is not hard to follow the successive targets of indebtedness, each producing a bubble and each finally collapsing. The first big one was the OPEC-induced large oil price rises in 1973 and 1979. The OPEC price rise was sponsored not by the radical members of OPEC but by Saudi Arabia and Iran (of the Shah), the two closest allies of the United States among the OPEC members. There has long been reason to believe that the United States encouraged their moves.

In any case, the financial consequences of the oil price rises were clear. A great deal of money flowed into the coffers of the OPEC countries. This had a double negative effect on non-oil-exporting states in the South and the socialist bloc. They had to pay more for the needed oil and all products made with oil, and their export income was reduced because of the recession in North America and western Europe. The balance of payments difficulties of these countries were leading to popular unrest.

The OPEC countries could not utilize immediately all of the increased income and deposited the rest in Western banks. The banks sent emissaries to the countries of the South and the socialist bloc to offer them loans to alleviate the balance of payments difficulties, which almost all of them readily accepted. These countries found it difficult, however, to keep up with repayments to the banks, eventually causing the so-called debt crisis. It was publicly signaled by Mexico's default in 1982. Actually, however, it really started with Poland's near default in 1980. The austerity measures that the Polish government put into effect in order to make debt payments were the trigger for Solidarność.

The next set of debtors was the wave of large corporations which, beginning in the 1980s, issued the famous junk bonds as a means of overcoming their liquidity problems. This led to acquisitions by a group of ravenous investors, who made their money by stripping the enterprises of material value. The 1990s saw the beginning of extensive individual indebtedness, especially in the North, made possible by extensive use of credit cards and then later investment in housing. The first decade of the 21st century saw the remarkable rise in public indebtedness of the United States resulting from the combination of enormous war costs and large-scale reduction in tax income. With the collapse of the US housing market in 2007, the world's press and politicians took public note of a "crisis," the efforts to "bail out" the banks and, in the case of the United States, to print currency. This was followed by the ever-widening circle of indebtednesses of governments, leading to pressures everywhere for austerity measures to reduce state debt, which reductions simultaneously have reduced effective demand.

The first decade of the 21st century has also seen the geographic reloca-tion of capital appropriation. The rise of the so-called emergent countries, notably the BRICS (Brazil, Russia, India, China, and South Africa), is the kind of slow reordering of the hierarchy of the modern world-system that has been seen regularly before. However, this presumes that there is room in the system for new productive leading industries, something the general-ized profit squeeze seems to counterindicate. Rather, the rise of the BRICS has involved a widening of the numbers of persons involved in partaking of the distribution of world surplus value. This actually reduces, not increases, the possibilities of the endless accumulation of capital, and intensifies rather than counteracts the structural crisis of the world-system. Furthermore, the austerity measures now so widespread are reducing the customer base for the exports of the BRICS.

The most likely financial result of the economic turmoil will be the final eviction of the United States dollar as the world's reserve currency, followed not by another currency performing this function, but a multicurrency world that allows for the constant fluctuations of exchange rates, a further inducement to the freezing of the financing of new productive activity.

Meanwhile, and simultaneously, the decline of US hegemony became irreparable after the blowback caused by the political-military fiasco of the neocon program of unilateral military machismo undertaken in the period 2001–2006 by the administration of President George W. Bush. The out-come has been the reality of a multipolar world, in which there are eight to ten centers of power, sufficiently strong that they can negotiate with other centers with relative autonomy. However, there are now too many centers of power. One consequence is the frequent tentative geopolitical realignments, as each of these centers seeks maximum advantage. Fluctu-ating markets and currencies are thereby reinforced by fluctuating power alliances.

The basic reality is unpredictability not merely in some middle run but very much in the short run. The sociopsychological consequences of this short-run unpredictability have been confusion, anger, disparagement of those in power, and above all acute fear. This fear leads to the search for political alternatives of kinds not entertained before. The media refer to this as populism, but it is far more complicated than this slogan term suggests. For some the fear leads to multiple and irrational scapegoatings. For others, it leads to the willingness to unthink deeply ingrained assumptions about the operations of the modern world-system. This can be seen in the United States as the difference between the Tea Party movement and the Occupy Wall Street movement.

The main concern of every government in the world—from the United States to China, from France to Russia to Brazil, not to speak of all the weaker governments on the world scene—has become the urgency of averting an uprising of unemployed workers joined by middle strata whose savings and pensions are disappearing. One reaction has been that the governments have all become protectionist (while vigorously denying this). The reason for this protectionist thrust is that governments are seeking to obtain short-term money, however they can and at whatever price they have to pay. Since protectionism is insufficient to overcome unemployment, governments are also becoming more repressive.

This combination of austerity, repression, and the search for short-term money makes the global situation even worse. It accounts for an ever-tighter gridlock of the system. Gridlock in turn will result in ever-wilder fluctuations, and will consequently make short-term predictions—both economic and political—ever more unreliable. And this in turn will aggravate the popular fears and alienation. It is a negative cycle.

The Political Struggle over the Replacement System

The question before the world today is not in what way governments can reform the capitalist system such that it can renew its ability to pursue effectively the endless accumulation of capital. There is no way to do this. The question therefore has become what will replace this system. And this is a question both for the 1% and the 99%, in the language used since 2011. Of course, not everyone agrees, or phrases it this way. Indeed, most people still assume that the system is continuing, using the old rules, perhaps after amending the rules. This is not wrong. It is just that, in the present situations, using the old rules actually intensifies the structural crisis.

There are however some actors who are quite aware of the structural crisis. They are aware that while we cannot maintain the present system, we can contribute to deciding which prong of the bifurcation the world will take, what kind of new historical system the world will construct. Whether we acknowledge it or not, we are living amidst a struggle for the successor system. While complexity studies insists that the outcome of such a bifurcation is intrinsically unpredictable, nonetheless the options between which the world will choose are quite straightforward, and can be sketched in broad terms.

One kind of possible new stable system is one that retains the basic features of the present system: hierarchy, exploitation, and polarization. Capitalism is far from the only kind of system that can have such features, and the new one could be far worse than capitalism. The logical alternative to this is a system that is relatively democratic and relatively egalitarian. This latter has never yet existed; it is only a possibility. Of course, none of us can design either alternative in institutional detail. Such a design will evolve as the new system begins its life.

I have given symbolic names to the two possibilities. I call them "the spirit of Davos" and "the spirit of Porto Alegre." The names themselves are unimportant. What we need to analyze are the probable organizational strategies on each side in this struggle that started more or less in the 1970s and will continue in all probability to circa 2040 or 2050.

The political struggles of a structural crisis have two basic characteristics. First, there is a fundamental change of the situation from that of the "normal" operation of an historical system. During "normal" life, there exists a very strong pressure to return to equilibrium. That is what makes it "normal." But in a structural crisis, the fluctuations are wide and constant, and the system is ever further from equilibrium. This is the definition of a structural crisis. It follows that however radical are "revolutions," during "normal" times their effect is limited. In contrast, during a structural crisis, small social mobilizations have very great effects. This is the so-called butterfly effect, when free will prevails over determinism.

The second politically significant characteristic of a structural crisis is that neither alternative "spirit" can be organized such that a small group can fully determine its actions. There are multiple players, representing different interests, believing in different short-run tactics, and coordination among them is difficult to achieve. Furthermore, the militants on each side must spend energy persuading the always larger group of potential supporters of the utility of their actions. It is not only the system that is chaotic. The struggle for the successor system is also chaotic.

What we can perceive, up to now, are the strategies that have been emerging in practice. The camp of the "spirit of Davos" is deeply divided. One group favors immediate and long-term harsh repression, and has invested its resources in organizing a network of armed enforcers to crush opposition. There is however another group who feel that repression can never work over the long term. They favor the di Lampedusa strategy of changing everything so that nothing changes. They talk about meritocracy, green capitalism, more equity, more diversity, and an open hand to the rebellious—all in the spirit of heading off a system premised on relative democracy and relative equality.

The camp of the "spirit of Porto Alegre" is similarly split.

There are those whose tactics for the transition period reflect their image of the world they want to build. It is sometimes called "horizontalism." In practice, it seeks to maximize debate and the search for relative consensus among persons of divergent backgrounds and immediate interests. It is a search to institutionalize a functional decentralization of the movement and the world. And this group has also emphasized the reality of what is often called a "civilizational crisis," by which is really meant a rejection of the basic objective of economic growth and substituting for this objective the search for rational balances of social objectives that will result precisely in relative democracy and relative egalitarianism.

Arrayed against them is the group that insists that, in a struggle for political power, vertical organization of some kind is a *sine qua non*, without which the group is doomed to failure. This group also emphasizes the importance of achieving significant short-run economic growth in the less "developed" areas of the present-day world in order to have the wherewithal to redistribute benefits.

Thus the picture is not one of a simple two-sided struggle but rather of a political field with four groups. And that is very confusing to everyone. The confusion is at one and the same time intellectual, moral, and political. And this reinforces the uncertainty of the outcome.

Finally, this kind of uncertainty heightens the short-run problems of the existing system. Such uncertainty is both exhilarating (the feeling that action makes a difference) and paralyzing (the sense that we can't move since the short-run consequences are so uncertain). This is true both for those who benefit from the existing system (the capitalists) and those who are the vast underclasses.

So, to resume, the modern world-system in which we are living cannot continue because it has moved too far from equilibrium, and no longer permits capitalists to accumulate capital endlessly. Nor do the underclasses any longer believe that history is on their side, and that their descendants will necessarily inherit the world. We are consequently living in a structural crisis in which there is a struggle about the successor system. Although the outcome is unpredictable, we can feel sure that one side or the other will win out in the coming decades, and a new reasonably stable world-system (or set of world-systems) will be established. What we can all do is try to analyze the historical options, make our moral choice about the preferred outcome, and evaluate the optimal political tactics to get there.

History is on nobody's side. We all may misjudge how we should act. Since the outcome is inherently, and not extrinsically, unpredictable, we have at best a 50–50 chance of getting the kind of world-system we prefer. But 50–50 is a lot, not a little.

2

THE END OF MIDDLE-CLASS WORK: NO MORE ESCAPES

Randall Collins

A long-term structural weakness of capitalism is now coming to the fore. It is the technological displacement of labor by machinery, which for the last twenty years has taken the form of computerization and information technology. This displacement is now accelerating and threatening the existence of the middle class. My argument is not very original. Marx also had a technological displacement mechanism, based on factory machinery, although in his argument it is combined with a number of other theoretical mechanisms, including business cycles, falling rates of profit, and—in current Neo-Marxian theories—financialization and financial crisis. What I want to emphasize, however, is that the process of technological displacement of labor, driven to a sufficient extreme, will generate the long-term and quite possibly terminal crisis of capitalism, all by itself and without the other processes in Marxian and Neo-Marxian theory. Business cycles may be hazy and imprecise in their timing and variable in the height and depth of their swings, as are Kondratieff waves and world-system hegemonies on the global level. Financial crises may be contingent and avoidable through the right policy. No matter. The structural crisis of technological displacement transcends cycles and financial bubbles. It is the deep threat to the future of capitalism. Yes, there are short-term crises driven by financial, cyclical and other mechanisms; but what I focus upon here is a long-term structural shift, one that very likely will bring capitalism to an end within the next thirty to fifty years.

I make no claims for the purity or authenticity of the lesson that I borrow from Marx. Sociology today, if it believes in anything, believes in multiple processes, multiple causes, and multiple paradigms for dealing with our chosen aspects of the world. In an important sense, in sociology Weber has triumphed over Marx, and we all talk about the interpenetration of class, politics, and culture, and of gender too. Nevertheless, there are moments when the key feature of long-term structural change is at issue—above all the issue of structural crisis. Here, for all our multidisciplinarity and our celebration of intellectual diversity, is an occasion when it seems to me one line of theory stands head and shoulders above all others in dealing with the mechanisms of crisis and the direction of very long-term structural change. The theory I will extol is a stripped-down version of the fundamental insight that Marx and Engels had formulated already in the 1840s.

It is a stripped-down Marxism indeed. No labor theory of value, no reference to expropriation of labor from the means of production, no alienation from species-being. It makes no ontological claims and does not posit any final emancipation at the end of the crisis. I have stripped it down to a theory of long-term economic crisis; we need other lines of sociology for what happens in response to the crisis, and what arises politically and socially afterward. Moreover, it is not a theory of the conquest of the state as result of economic crisis, not by itself alone a theory of revolution—although at the end I will discuss what sociologists have learned about the causes of revolution. And although it has implications for the future of socialism, it is not a theory of socialism and what would make socialism work better in the future than it did in the past. No, it is a theory of crisis first and foremost.

Technological displacement is the mechanism by which innovations in equipment and organization save labor, thereby enabling fewer employed persons to produce more at lower cost. Marx and Engels argued that capitalists strive to increase profit in competition with each other; those who fail to do so are driven out of the market. But as labor-saving machinery replaces workers, unemployment grows and consumer demand falls. Technology promises abundance, but the potential product cannot be sold because too few persons have enough income to buy it. Extrapolating this underlying structural tendency, Marx and Engels predicted the downfall of capitalism and its replacement by socialism.

Why has this not happened in the 160 years since the theory was formulated? As is well known, where socialist regimes have come into power, the transition was not driven by capitalist economic crisis—nor indeed when they have fallen out of power. My point here is the absence of definitive capitalist breakdown through technological displacement. Marx and Engels focused on the displacement of working-class labor; they did not foresee the rise of the massive middle class of white-collar employees, of administrative and clerical workers and educated professionals. But this is why I now argue for the return of technological displacement crisis. Until the 1980s or 1990s, mechanization chiefly displaced manual labor. In the most recent wave of technology, we now have the displacement of administrative labor, the downsizing of the middle class. Information technology is the technology of communications, and it has launched the second great era of contraction of work, the displacement of communicative labor, which is what middle-class employees do. Mechanization is now joined by robotization and electronicization—an ugly and ungainly term to add to our vocabulary of ugly terms dictating our long-term future.

As the working class shrunk through mechanization, capitalism was saved by the rise of the middle class. Now computerization, the Internet, and the wave of new micro-electronic devices are beginning to squeeze out the middle class. Can capitalism survive this second wave of technological displacement?

In the past, capitalism has escaped from technological displacement crises by five main escape routes. I will argue that all five of these now are becoming blocked—dead ends.

ESCAPE NUMBER 1: NEW TECHNOLOGY CREATES NEW JOBS AND ENTIRE NEW JOB SECTORS

Pessimism about new technology has long been considered futile and wrongheaded. The Luddites in 1811 who broke machines that destroyed the jobs of handicraft workers did not see that their system of production was giving way to a factory system which would vastly expand industries and increase, for over a century, the numbers of factory workers. Development theory, formulated in the mid-20th century, held that the natural tendency is to move through the stages of primary, secondary, and tertiary labor sectors (i.e., extractive, manufacturing, and administrative or service work). But development theory was just an empirical generalization from a particular time in history; there is no guarantee that this process will go on forever. Agricultural labor went from a large majority of all jobs to about 1% in today's advanced economies; manufacturing went from a height of some 40% to 15% or less. These figures show the magnitude of what technological displacement can do. A similar reduction in the administrative/service sector is plausible.

Schumpeter, the best theorist of capitalist innovation, theorizes that new products—and hence the major sources of profit—come on the market by reorganizing the factors of production into new combinations; this always involves what Schumpeter called "creative destruction." Nevertheless, Schumpeter-inspired economists also rely on nothing more than extrapolation of past trends for the argument that the number of jobs created by new products will make up for the jobs lost by destruction of old markets.

None of these theories take account of the technological displacement of communicative labor, the escape valve that in the past has brought new employment to compensate for the loss of old employment. It has been argued that as telephone operators and file clerks lose their jobs to automated and computerized systems, an equal number acquire jobs as software developers, computer technicians, and mobile phone salespersons. But no one has shown any good theoretical reason why these numbers should be equal; much less why the automation of these kinds of technical and communicative tasks—for instance by shopping online—cannot drive down the size of the white-collar labor force. Technological displacement is ongoing as we speak. Within the past few years, checkout clerks in stores have been replaced by automated self-serve checkouts, cutting into one of the largest areas of lower-middle class service sector employment. At a higher skill level, professional journalists are being displaced by the downsizing or disappearance of newspapers, driven by competition from online news, itself deriving from a small number of paid journalists and a large number of amateur, unpaid bloggers.

Computerization of the middle class is not being compensated by the creation of new jobs at an equal rate. New jobs are created, but they do not match the number of jobs eliminated, nor do they replace lost income. This is a reason why job-retraining programs for displaced workers have failed to affect the rate of structural unemployment. Computerization and the Internet have generated new sectors of work: software design, website construction, numerous work-from-home online informational and consulting services. These latter tend to be low paying, not surprising given easy access by a growing number of competitors, many of whom provide their offerings for free. Although Information Technology (IT) generates new activities, it does not generate paying jobs at the same rate that it eliminates them. The proliferation of opinion blogs does not make up for the elimination of paid occupations in journalism.

Focusing solely on the paid employment generated by IT as compared to the jobs displaced by IT, and extrapolating trends over a period of decades, is it plausible that 70% or more of world employment will be computer programmers and designers of software and computer applications? Bear in mind that computerization is still in its youth, past its infancy but not yet into maturity. The metaphor is overly biological, but the point is that more sophisticated computation is still to come: Artificial Intelligence, in which machines take over higher cognitive processes from humans. When computer programming itself is done entirely by computers, as well as the creation of new applications, the displacement of middle-class labor will be nearly complete. Jobs for computer programmers will no longer be an escape route. It never has been an equalizer compensating for the numbers of jobs lost; and over time, the amount of job creation for humans compared to work taken over by computers will be a steadily decreasing slice—a channel whose walls grow steadily narrower.

In an advanced economy such as the United States, jobs in the service sector have grown to about 75% of the labor force, a result of the decline in industrial and agricultural/extractive occupations (Autor and Dorn 2013). But the service sector is becoming squeezed by the IT economy, itself little more than twenty-five years old. Sales jobs are rapidly becoming automated by computer-generated messaging and by online buying; in brick-and-mortar stores, retail clerks are being replaced by electronic scanners. Management positions too will come under increasing pressure as artificial intelligence grows.

There is no intrinsic end to this process of replacing human with computers and other machines. The displacement of human work will go on, not just for the next twenty years but the next hundred, even the next thousand years—unless something extrinsic happens to change the underlying mechanism driving technological displacement of work: capitalist competition.

The future world run by computers will not necessarily be that depicted by George Orwell in *Nineteen Eighty-Four*, where high tech is used for surveillance and autocratic state control. Orwell missed the economic dimension: how electronic high technology affects not just politics but employment. Similarly with the benign version of the future depicted in space age adventure films, the question of who owns the robots and computers never comes up. In the real world, the answer is: the big computer systems will be (and are) owned by big capitalist property-holders. The manufacture of IT hardware as well as software is capitalist enterprise. The popular communications companies (Facebook, Google, Amazon, Twitter, and whatever their names will be over the coming decades) show the same pattern as the historical development of any other form of capitalist enterprise: rapid innovation chained to other innovations, proliferation of competitors, winnowing out of many through the growth of a few, enthusiastic investment by financial markets, then financial pressure and collapse of former front-runners. Consolidation into oligopoly in the IT era happens just as it did in previous waves of new technology. Since the IT period is still quite new, it isn't yet clear whether the pace toward oligopoly is different than in the era of the railroads or the era of the automobile industry; so far it looks like the current speed toward oligopoly is much faster than in previous periods. (This is a side question from the main issue of technological displacement of the middle class; as long as that goes on, whether there is a high degree of oligopoly or not does not much affect the long-term crisis of capitalism.)

But, one might object, Information Technology is different. Computerization is not just something that happens to big companies and big employers; it is something that ordinary people use and enjoy. Computers are not owned just by the capitalists; they are owned by all of us. That is like saying (in 1925 or 1955): automobiles are not capitalist industries; since I own one myself, I have the freedom to drive all over, escape, get laid in the back seat, drag-race on the highway if I want to. Enthusiasm for products of capitalist industry is part of what makes capitalism successful. That's fine; enjoy it while you can. The fact that you can hear portable music at any time and place, post and view images and texts and all the other things that consumer IT devices enable contemporary consumers to do—all this says nothing about whether or not there are jobs for persons like yourself. The popularity of automobiles was not just consumer enjoyment; it reflected an industry which, for several decades, generated a large number of well-paying jobs. Subsequently, technological displacement and capitalist consolidation have drastically reduced jobs in the automotive sector. All the personal electronic devices of today that absorb people's attention and enthusiasm will not fend off capitalist crisis, if these same consumers cannot find jobs. Eventually they will not be able to buy these devices, nor their producers to sell them. That is the shape of deep, structural capitalist crisis.

ESCAPE NUMBER 2: GEOGRAPHICAL SPREAD OF MARKETS

We tend to think of market spread as globalization, but globalization is only a quantitative difference in degree, not a qualitative difference in kind. Even within the confines of state borders, markets have grown by spreading to regions where a product was initially unknown; thus local conditions favored profit for the innovator coming from elsewhere. Geographical spread works in tandem with product innovation, keeping up the ongoing existence of market frontiers. Dynamic markets always have the buzz of newness, the cultural prestige of being a center or keeping up with a center, or the negative prestige of striving to escape from backwardness. The liberal version of this mechanism, on the global or interstate scale, is modernization theory or development theory; each part of the world successively ascends the stages, until presumably all will be fully developed, tertiary-sector service economies. We are now seeing this come into being, the argument goes, in India and China, the big nations of the Third World making their way inexorably to modernity.

The Neo-Marxist version of this process is World-System theory [Arrighi 1994; Chase-Dunn 1989; Wallerstein 1974–2011]. This is a less benign version of the geographical spread of capitalist markets; world market domination is buttressed by military power and political influence; the hegemonic center exploits the labor or raw materials of the periphery, with the aid of a transmission belt of semiperipheral regions. World-system theory complicates the pattern by a succession of hegemonies marked by major wars, and keyed to long Kondratieff waves of relative expansion and stagnation in world markets. But these cycles of serial hegemons—Spain, Holland, Britain, the United States, conjecturally China—logically come to an end when the periphery is exhausted, and every region of the globe is fully brought into the capitalist market. There are no more safety-valves, no more regions for exploitation; capitalist profit dries up.

Leaving aside the specific merits of world-system theory predictions, the point I would emphasize is that globalization of markets is now undercutting middle-class jobs. Internet technology makes it possible for white-collar workers in India—or anywhere else—to compete for jobs in servicing computerized businesses in the core capitalist regions of the world. Whereas in the past middle-class workers have been protected from competition to a greater degree than manual workers, this is no longer true; the Internet creates a much wider pool of workers who can access available jobs, especially if they do not have to physically move to a distant place of work. Contemporary globalization also involves much more rapid international travel. Managerial and professional workers physically move their expertise and their negotiating skills to entrepreneurial sites around the globe; this has the further effect of homogenizing upper-middle-class labor into a single labor market, raising the prospects of cheapening management costs, and displacing even high-level technocratic labor. Greater connectedness leads to greater competition for jobs, undercutting middle-class salaries. This process is relatively recent; the jet-set boom of the upper-middle class in recent decades is becoming vulnerable to the same structural displacement that the cost-cutting experts have visited upon their employees. High-level professional and technical specialists face a much more competitive and uncertain existence than ever before, when they were protected by national enclaves.

In the past, international migration provided cheap labor for centers of manufacturing, and more recently for the lower levels of the advanced service economies, thereby undercutting the working class of wealthier nations. Now as communications technology tends to spread cultural capital more homogeneously around the globe, it is middle- and upper-middle-class labor that is being undercut.

Escape Number 3: Meta-markets in Finance

If working-class and then middle-class labor are technologically displaced, can the slack be taken up by everyone becoming a capitalist? This argument has been advanced as employee pension funds have come to play a large role in financial markets, and as financial services firms have expanded and have aggressively marketed investments to a larger constituency. In countries like the United States, where home ownership is widespread, the inflation of housing prices brought opportunities not only to treat home ownership as a speculative investment, but to withdraw equity from inflated housing prices in the form of cash for consumer spending. These financial practices have been among the short-term sources of the recent economic crisis and especially the financial meltdown of 2008.

I am not proposing that our recent problems are the beginning of the end of capitalism. We will no doubt ride out this crisis, like other crises, in the short run, while leaving a certain amount of long-term damage. Financial crisis has been widely discussed. What I want to examine here is not short-run crises but the contributions of financialization to the displacement of middle-class labor.

Recent financial manipulations are examples of a deeper structural tendency in capitalism: the pyramiding of meta-markets upon each other in financial markets. Capitalism, ever since it entered its phase of self-sustaining growth or internally driven expansion, has connected markets for material goods and services with markets for financial instruments. Schumpeter [1939] defined entrepreneurial capitalism as enterprise carried out with borrowed money. Static markets merely reproduce existing stocks and workforces, unless new combinations are taken out of the circular flow of reproduction; this is done by borrowing against the future. Thus in Schumpeter's [1911] view, banks are the headquarters of the capitalist system, deciding where new allocations for development will be made. But since financing is intrinsically speculative, its relationship with existing material arrangements can vary enormously. The upper atmosphere of the financial system can have many multiples of the value of what is actually bought and sold in material goods and services; we see this, for instance, in the vast amounts of money in international currency speculation in relation to the size of GDP, or the extraordinarily inflated sums in hedge funds, especially before the 2008 crash.

By pyramiding meta-markets I mean the historical tendency for any given financial market to give rise to a higher-order market in lower-order financial instruments. In real social practices, all monies are promises to pay in the future. Thus financial specialists can create promises to pay promises to pay, and so on up to almost any level of complexity. Loans, liens, equities, bonds, all these are relatively low levels of pyramiding. Short-selling stock market shares, bundling mortgages for secondary resale markets, leveraged buyouts, mutual funds, hedge funds, and other complex trading schemes are higher-order markets built upon the instruments of exchange. There is in principle no upper limit to how many layers can be added. Very large sums can be generated at higher levels, although the conversion of these monies into low-level goods and services is problematic. The illusion is created because they are all designated by the same unit of account—dollars, pounds, Euros—but these nominal amounts can rise so high that cashing them out in the real material world is literally impossible.

Pyramided financial markets have a high degree of social constructedness. Of course almost everything is socially constructed in some way, but some are much more remotely connected to material constraints than others. An army, for instance, has an important degree of social constructedness, especially in combat, where, as Napoleon said, the moral is to the material as three to one; nevertheless, an army with five times the size and weaponry of its opponent will almost always win, provided it maintains some minimal degree of social cohesion. In the world of pyramided financial instruments, the moral (i.e., the interactional processes of the network and its emotional moods) is to the material economy as something on the order of from six to one (which is the ratio between money loaned out and actual bank deposits) up to quite possibly hundreds to one in highly leveraged financial manipulations. As sociologists, we need to look at social constructedness not as a philosophical constant but as a set of variations, which can be theorized both in their static relationship to network structures, and in their dynamics of boom and bust over time.

My chief point here is that the more pyramided financial meta-markets are, the more volatile and crisis-prone they are, with booms and busts far out of proportion to what is happening in the low-level material economy. But there is an optimistic side as well—optimistic if you would like to preserve capitalism. Financial markets are intrinsically flexible, like giant balloons made out of magic material that can inflate to any size at all. This lends plausibility to the idea that everyone can become a finance capitalist, playing the great game of financial markets. And indeed popular participation in financial markets has grown a good deal during the late 20th century and the early 21st, through employee pension funds, millions of small stock market investors, and speculating through mortgaged home ownership in the Ponzi scheme of the inflationary housing market.

How far can this go? Can it save capitalism? It would surely be a rocky road, given the inherent volatility of financial markets, their tendency to booms and busts. This has been a long-term historical pattern, ever since the Dutch tulip investment mania in 1637 and the South Sea bubble in 1720. Speculative collapses have been so common that Schumpeter [1939] regarded business cycles as intrinsic to capitalism, and their presence a historical marker of the existence of self-driven capitalist dynamics. One could turn the historical argument around; speculative busts have always bottomed out and eventually financial markets have gone up again. Financial crises are in the nature of the capitalist beast, and the historical record suggests that we will always recover from any financial crisis. Again we have an empirical generalization without good theoretical basis. What happens when financial crisis is coupled with structural depletion of middle-class jobs, and a technological displacement crisis throughout virtually the entire labor force? Can income from the financial sector reach so far that it supplants salaries and wages as the primary source of income for everyone?

There are two possibilities here: either everyone becomes a capitalist living off of investment returns, or the financial sector itself becomes the major area of employment (i.e., the growth of financial labor). Taking the first of these, it is hard to envision a future in which everyone lives as a financial investor. It takes some initial accumulation of funds for your initial bankroll in order to start investing, the gambling stakes to get into the game. Small investors get started with their salaries, savings, and pensions; but these are just what would dry up under the technological displacement scenario. We are at the theoretical frontier here, and the future of political economy may well include things undreamed of in your philosophy, Horatio. But is it conceivable that in the future when everything is automated that entire populations will spend their lives as financial investors, a reserve army of gamblers in lifelong casinos? Not everyone goes on making money throughout their investment career; some people lose their investments even in good times, and during a speculative bust many people do. And once they wash out of the speculative market, do they ever get back in, barring gainful employment on their own?

Financial markets are intrinsically inegalitarian, concentrating wealth in the small number of big players at the top of the pyramid. It is precisely the advantage of better networking, insider viewpoint, first-mover advantages, and ability to ride out fluctuations better than small players that gives big players in higher meta-markets their capacity to make profits from the medium and small players in lower-order markets. Pyramided levels of monies illustrate Viviana Zelizer's [1994] theory that money is not homogeneous but plural, diverse sets of specific currencies circulating within their own social networks. Those who play in the circuit of hedge funds, for instance, are a very restricted group of persons and organizations; small players are not even legally allowed into these markets. Perhaps this is beside the point; in the idyllic financial utopia of the future, core investors will become mega-rich, but smaller investors will get their share. Will this be enough to sustain consumer spending throughout the entire economy and thus keep the machinery of capitalism going? Not if financial markets tend toward ever-greater concentration, exploiting the smaller participants at the bottom.

For the second possibility: technological displacement can be expected to make inroads into employment in the financial sector. As I mentioned in the optimistic capitalist scenario, the financial market can prop up an otherwise diminishing middle class either by making everyone a capitalist, or making everyone an employee of the financial sector. Is this latter plausible—when all other work is technologically displaced, financial work will take up the slack? But why should technological displacement not take place within financial employment itself? We have seen a low-level version of this already, with online banking eliminating bank tellers and clerks, and banks downsizing their workforces even as they handle larger amounts of monetary instruments. The mantra of capitalist economists is that unskilled labor is displaced by more highly skilled professionals. But how far can the sector of financial professionals expand? Temporary run-ups such as seen during the 1990s may well prove to be a passing phase; and in any case it is hard to imagine that anything near a majority of workers in an automated future will have jobs as hedge fund managers. Still, this may be the best dream future capitalism has to offer—no one doing any real productive labor, everyone living as a financial manipulator. Maybe we will experience a phase of this, sometime later on in the 21st century; if so I would predict it will be the run-up to the last crash of capitalism.

Escape Number 4: Government Employment and Investment

Now we come to escape routes that are not intrinsic to capitalism itself, but salvation from outside. Prominent among them is the Keynesian welfare-state solution. It was widely argued fifty years ago that capitalism was saved by the welfare states of the 1930s, 1940s, and 1950s—the liberal Left saving capitalism when the ideological Right proved incapable of saving itself. Can government spending solve the technological displacement of the middle class?

The main form of direct government hiring has been middle-class administrative jobs; thus any continuation of the trend to automate and computerize such jobs would contract government employment too. A sufficiently resolute political regime could resist this by refusing to automate jobs away. This kind of neo-Luddite policy was tried by British unions and socialist politicians from the late 1940s through the 1970s. Staying technologically backward for the sake of protecting employment would probably be demoralizing and politically unviable; it was this atmosphere in Britain that led to the Thatcherite reaction. Another version that has worked in the past has been military Keynesianism, the buildup of employment in military forces along with stimulating the economy through military production. But the contemporary military has gone high tech, promoting transformation into smaller fighting forces coordinated by computers, satellites, aerial sensors, and remote control surveillance and targeting devices. The military is the leading edge of robotization, and it is doubtful that even a World War-style all-out mobilization would ever produce the kind of massive militaries seen in the 20th century.

Besides direct government employment, there is government spending, the favorite tool of today's stimulus packages. Most of those invest in material infrastructure—roads, bridges, airports, energy, as well as the so-called information highway. But these areas too undergo computerization and automation, adding to the trend of technological displacement. Even less likely to stem the tide of job displacement is government investment in the private sector. Especially with the mantra to carry out such investments efficiently, government assumes the role of capitalist or at least capitalist overseer, all too willing to cut labor costs, and therefore to cut employment.

Another version of market intervention is regulation of the private marketplace, mandating a shorter work week, and protecting jobs from cuts.

These policies have been widely practiced by Continental European states, but have not done much more than slow the drift to technological displacement. On the whole, such policies tend to protect existing jobholders, but to freeze out youth. That problem could be solved by government deliberately hiring youth in massive numbers; this has rarely been attempted (except in the military version), although in Escape #5 I will suggest that this has been done surreptitiously through inflating educational credentialing.

In principle, political policies could do anything whatsoever, constrained only by political will, which is to say mobilized political power and its vision as set by political cultures. Obviously political cultures have a long way to go from here if the state is going to do anything significant about technological displacement of the middle class. Mixed "liberal" government policies propping up the private economy can keep capitalism limping along quite a way into the future. But the mixed approach is not likely to solve the long-term problem of technological displacement, as long as private profitmaking drives the economy.

We need to think of the pressure, not merely in present-day (US) terms of 10% unemployment with small fluctuations of a few percentage points, but into the computerized future where the base unemployment rate could be three or five times higher. In other words, a situation of massive employment crisis, and governments elected to take action by the welfare state pathway. Obstacles to this are easy to envision, since they fill the political sphere at present. One is the antitax movement, likely to continue strongly among small businesses including struggling Internet entrepreneurs, as the Internet exposes them to heavy competition. These push against government acting to bolster employment, thus contributing to system crisis. On the other side is the demand from political constituencies—above all the unemployed and underemployed, who are now coming increasingly from the ranks of the educated and therefore highly mobilizable population.

Contending forces are in play. Which ones will win, and to what extent? Unrestricted free-market capitalism, left to itself, has no way of heading off such crisis. Its favorite reforms—reducing taxes and government regulation, encouraging capitalists to engage in still further expansion in any way they wish—all have the effect of pushing technological displacement, as well as generating other kinds of problems including financial manipulations and crises. The pro-welfare state forces in principle may have a solution to unemployment, but they run up against the budgetary problems of the state.

A state which funds an expensive welfare state opens itself up to the pressure of financial markets, risking destruction of the purchasing power of its currency. Thus it would appear that a welfare state policy is caught in a damned-if-you-do, damned-if-you-don't position. But let us see this in a long-term perspective, not just as an immediate stumbling block in everyday politics. A state caught in a deep structural dilemma is moving toward a revolutionary breakdown of the system. The fiscal crisis of the state is one of the main components of state breakdown; we need only add the other two components, a split between state elites over which solution to seek, and mobilization of a radical movement from outside. The split between state elites here just means a radicalization of the opposition between those who maintain their alliance to the financial markets, and those who are committed to using the state to alleviate unemployment and inequality. In the context of 10% unemployment and a limping post-recession economy, polarization between these positions is not strong. But if we extrapolate this to 50% unemployment, and the deep depression sure to accompany it, the chances for full-scale state breakdown will be strong. At this point, a revolutionary overturn of the property system will be the most obvious solution, including seizing control of the financial system so that it cannot destroy a government's own currency. Not just particular features of capitalism, but its institutional underpinnings, would give way.

Escape Number 5: Educational Credential Inflation, and Other Hidden Keynesianism

Credential inflation is the rise in educational requirements for jobs as a rising proportion of the population attains more advanced degrees. The value of a given educational certificate or diploma declines as more people have one, thereby motivating them to stay in school longer. In the United States, high-school (i.e., twelve-year secondary school) diplomas were comparatively rare before World War II; now high-school degrees are so commonplace that their job value is worthless. University attendance is now over 60% of the youth cohort, and is on the way to the same fate as the high-school degree. It is a worldwide trend; in South Korea, 80% of high-school graduates now go on to higher education. The main thing that inflated degrees are worth is to plough them back into the educational market, seeking still higher degrees. This in principle is an endless process; it could very well reach the situation of the Chinese mandarin class during the later dynasties [Chaffee 1985], when students continued sitting for exams into their thirties and forties—only now this would affect the vast majority of the population instead of a small elite. Different countries have gone through educational inflation at different rates, but from the second half of the 20th century onward, all of them have followed this path [Brown and Bills 2011].

Educational degrees are a currency of social respectability, traded for access to jobs; like any currency, it inflates prices (or reduces purchasing power) when autonomously driven increases in monetary supply chase a limited stock of goods, in this case chasing an ever more contested pool of upper-middle-class jobs. Educational inflation builds on itself; from the point of view of the individual degree-seeker, the best response to its declining value is to get even more education. The more persons who hold advanced degrees, the more competition among them for jobs, and the higher the educational requirements that can be demanded by employers. This leads to renewed seeking of more education, more competition, and more credential inflation.

Within this overall inflationary process, the most highly educated segment of the population has received an increasingly greater proportion of the income; at least this has been so in the United States since the 1980s. One should be wary about extrapolating this particular historical period into an eternal pattern for all times and places. Those at the top of the inflationary competition for credentials have benefited from several processes: [a] they were in the relatively safe havens when technological displacement was hitting, initially, the last of the decently paid manual labor force, and then low-paid clerical work. [b] The quality of work performance between different levels of the educational hierarchy has apparently widened. What has been insufficiently recognized is that the inflationary spiral in schooling has brought increasing alienation and perfunctory performance among students who are not at the top of the competition, those who are forced to stay in school more years but get no closer to elite jobs. Grade inflation and low standards of promotion are symptoms of this process. There is considerable evidence, from ethnographies of teenagers, of youth culture, and especially youth gangs, that the expansion of schooling has brought increasing alienation from official adult standards [Milner 2004]. The first youth gangs appeared in the early 1950s when working-class youth were first being pressured into staying in school instead of going into the labor force; and their ideology was explicitly anti-school [Schneider 1999; Cohen 1955]. This is the source of the oppositional youth culture that has grown so widely, both among the minority who belong to gangs and the majority who share their antinomian stance. Employers today complain that jobs in the lower half of the service sector are hard to fill with reliable, conscientious employees. But this is not so much a failure of mass secondary education to provide good technical skills (one hardly needs high-school math and science to greet customers politely or ship packages to the right address) as a pervasive alienation from doing menial work. The mass inflationary school system tells its students that it is providing a pathway to elite jobs, but spills most of them into an economy where menial work is all that is available unless one has outcompeted 80% of one's school peers. No wonder they are alienated.

Although credential inflation is the primary mechanism of educational expansion, overt recognition of this process has been repressed from consciousness, in virtually a Freudian manner. In this case, the idealizing and repressing agent, the Superego of the educational world, is the prevailing technocratic ideology. Rising technical requirements of jobs drive out unskilled labor, the argument goes, and today's high-skilled jobs demand steadily increasing levels of education. Thirty years ago, in *The Credential Society* [Collins 1979], I assembled evidence to show that technological change is not the driving force in rising credential requirements. The content of education is not predominantly set by technological demand; most technological skills—including the most advanced ones—are learned on the job or through informal networks, and the bureaucratic organization of education at best tries to standardize skills innovated elsewhere. In updated research on credential inflation vis-à-vis technological change [Collins 2002; Brown and Bills 2011], I have seen nothing that overturns my conclusions published in 1979. It is true that a small proportion of jobs benefit from scientific and technical education, but that is not what is driving the massive expansion of education. It is implausible that in the future most persons will be scientists or skilled technicians. Indeed, the biggest area of job growth in rich countries has been low-skilled service jobs, where it is cheaper to hire human labor than to automate [Autor and Dorn 2013]. In the current US economy, one of the biggest growth sectors is tattoo parlors [Halnon and Cohen 2006]: a non-credentialed occupation, small-scale business, low-paying and thus far immune from corporate control—and selling emblems of alienation from mainstream culture.

Although educational credential inflation expands on false premises—the ideology that more education will produce more equality of opportunity, more high-tech economic performance, and more good jobs—it does provide some degree of solution to technological displacement of the middle class. Educational credential inflation helps absorb surplus labor by keeping more people out of the labor force; and if students receive a financial subsidy, either directly or in the form of low-cost (and ultimately unrepaid) loans, it acts as hidden transfer payments. In places where the welfare state is ideologically unpopular, the mythology of education supports a hidden welfare state. Add the millions of teachers in elementary, secondary, and higher education, and their administrative staffs, and the hidden Keynesianism of educational inflation may be said to virtually keep the capitalist economy afloat.

As long as the educational system can be somehow financed, it operates as hidden Keynesianism: a hidden form of transfer payments and pump-priming, the equivalent of New Deal make-work setting the unemployed to painting murals in post offices or planting trees in conservation camps. Educational expansion is virtually the only legitimately accepted form of Keynesian economic policy, because it is not overtly recognized as such. It expands under the banner of high technology and meritocracy—it is the technology that requires a more educated labor force. In a roundabout sense this is true: it is the technological displacement of labor that makes school a place of refuge from the shrinking job pool, although no one wants to recognize the fact. No matter—as long as the number of those displaced is shunted into an equal number of those expanding the population of students, the system will survive.

The rub is on the expense side. The two main ways to pay for schooling (at all levels: elementary, secondary, tertiary, and whatever further levels become added on) are either by government provision or by private purchase. Both of these come under pressure in times of economic downturn and squeezed government revenue. In the years around 2010, both in the United States and many other countries, the costs of public education became such a substantial proportion of government budgets (especially at the local level) that they gave rise to movements to cut educational spending. In Chile, for instance, where 50% of the youth cohort now attends university, there is a struggle between the organized students demanding free university education for all and administrators and tax conservatives who push an increasing proportion of higher education into the private market-place. Similar issues have roiled the student population in France and else-where. In the United States, where higher education is funded largely (and increasingly) by the students themselves and their families, there has been much concern over the amount of debt in the form of student loans—now (as of 2011) approaching 10% of GDP. If one extrapolates both the num-bers of students extending their stay in schools in response to technological displacement, and the proportion of the economy made up by student debt, one can see that another twenty years or so of technological displacement and credential inflation will become enormously expensive to the system as a whole. What would happen if student debt rose to 50% of GDP, or 100%?

Education is a major cost of government, and this tends to limit future expansion. With higher costs, there are pressures to privatize, shifting the burden of funding to students or parents; but this too faces a limit as the middle class is economically squeezed. By 2012, there was a wave of public-ity in the United States about what kinds of degrees are not worth the cost of acquiring them, in terms of the jobs one can get or one fails to get. Although one individual solution would simply be to drop out of the educational com-petition, the more popular choice among youth has been to seek specific vocational education, and there has been an upsurge of schools in areas like apparel design, computer programming, business, etc. But the shift to vo-cational education does not evade the dynamic of credential inflation, and we can predict increasing competition inside those vocational sectors, and rising inflation of vocational degrees. One indicator has been controversy, both in the political sphere and in accrediting and regulatory agencies, cri-tiquing the low rate of job success for such vocational students, and denying them access to government loans. That is to say, the inflated value of educa-tional degrees has become an explicit problem.

Information Technology is again being invoked as a solution. There is a rush toward university courses online, thereby achieving great economies of scale. Some of these are for sale, albeit at rates far lower than the cost of actual tuition at a bricks-and-mortar institution. Others are offered altruisti-cally for free. Neither method will hinder credential inflation; indeed, both add to it, by putting still more educated persons on the market. As of now, the new kinds of credentials are being labeled as distinct from university degrees, and in that sense not directly competing with them. This remains to be seen; in effect a new form of cheap educational currency is being created, alongside a more traditional and expensive educational currency. If educational currencies are strictly like money, Gresham's law would apply, and the cheap currency would drive out the expensive one. On the other hand, in economic sociology, as we know from Viviana Zelizer (1994) and Harrison White (2002), high-quality economic objects can exist in separate circuits alongside cheap ones, and that may well continue to be the case in the production of educational credentials.

The dilemma is this: efforts to make education cheaper have the effect of reducing employment in the educational sector itself; if a few famous universities monopolize teaching through online courses, and a few professors can do the vast amount of the teaching with electronic assistance, one more sector of employment becomes technologically displaced. The result is the same through the pathway of old-fashioned tax revolts; a short-term reduction in the population's tax burden has the roundabout effect of reducing jobs available for that same population.

Of the five escape routes from capitalist crisis, continued educational inflation seems to me the most plausible. An expanding educational system driven by credential inflation reaches a potential crisis point within the educational system itself. This is not necessarily final. One can envision a series of such plateaus, stopping and restarting as our secular faith in salvation through education goes through disillusionment and revival. But if this becomes increasingly government sustained, it amounts to socialism in the guise of education. It is conceivable that liberal governments might find their way to keep expanding educational systems, using them as a Keynesian safety valve, and a form of transfer payments from the capitalists and the diminishing sector of the employed, to sustain the otherwise unemployed. But to get such a government might well take a near-revolutionary disillusionment with capitalism.

WHEN WILL FULL-BLOWN CRISIS HAPPEN?

Computerization of middle-class labor (since the last decade of the 20th century) is proceeding at a much faster pace than the mechanization of the manual labor force (which took approximately the entire 19th century and three-quarters of the 20th). Technological displacement of middle-class labor is not much more than twenty years old; whereas it took almost 200 years to destroy the working-class labor force.

Another estimate of the timing of future capitalist crisis is provided by world-system (W-S) theory. In earlier writing on the capitalist world-system, Wallerstein and colleagues presented a theoretical model of systemic long cycles. The core regions of the W-S in their expansive phase generate their advantage by resources extracted under favorable conditions from the periphery. Hegemony is periodically threatened by conflicts within the core, and especially by semiperipheral zones rising to threaten the hegemon. Eventually the core gets caught up with, just as increasing competition in a new area of entrepreneurial profit brings down the profits once gained by the early innovator; in this respect, the W-S operates like Schumpeter's cycle of entrepreneurship, but on a global scale. With each new cycle, new opportunities for expansion and profit arise, under the leadership of a new hegemon. The crucial condition in the background, however, is that there must be an external area, outside the W-S, which can be incorporated and turned into the periphery of the system. Thus there is a final ending point to the W-S: when all the external areas have been penetrated. At this point the struggle for profit in the core and semiperiphery cannot be resolved by finding new economic regions to conquer. The W-S undergoes not just cyclical crisis but terminal transformation.

On the basis of past cycles, Wallerstein (also Arrighi, 1994) project the crisis of the W-S at approximately 2030–2045. My own estimate of the crisis point generated by the mechanism of technological displacement of the middle class depends on the rate at which structural unemployment grows. (This must be measured not merely in convenient technical terms such as, in the United States, the number of applications for unemployment compensation, but by our best measure of the proportion of the adult population unable to find work and driven out of the employment sector entirely.) An unemployment rate of 10% is painful, by American standards; 25% (found in crisis economies) is big trouble, but it has been sustained in the past. But when unemployment reaches 50% of the work-capable population, or 70%, the capitalist system must come under such pressure—both from underconsumption and political agitation—that it cannot survive. If we think such unemployment rates are unimaginable, let us imagine again, through the lens of technological displacement of all categories of work by electronic machinery. It is clear that the rate of technological displacement has accelerated in the last fifteen years. We could well reach 50% structural unemployment by the year 2040, and 70% not long after that. In gross terms, this agrees with the W-S projection of a terminal crisis of capitalism around the middle of the 21st century.

ANTI-CAPITALIST REVOLUTION: PEACEFUL OR VIOLENT?

If the crisis of technology displacement becomes severe enough—a highly automated, computerized world in which very few people work, and most of the population is unemployed or competing for menial low-paid service jobs—would there be a revolution?

Here we must leave economic crisis theory and examine theory of revolution. Since the 1970s, the theory of revolution has been revolutionized. Skocpol [1979], Goldstone [1991], Tilly [1995], and others, by their comparative researches on the rise and fall of state regimes, have established what can be called the state breakdown theory of revolution. Successful revolution depends on what happens at the top, not on disaffected and impoverished masses from below. The chief ingredients are: first, a fiscal crisis of the state; the state becomes unable to pay its bills, and above all to pay its security forces, its military and police. State fiscal crisis becomes lethal when it is joined by the second ingredient, a split among elites over how to deal with it. We could add secondary factors, back in the chain of antecedents, typically although not always including military causes; a state fiscal crisis often comes from accumulated military expenses, and elite deadlock is especially exacerbated by military defeat, which delegitimates government and provokes calls for drastic reform. Splits among elites paralyze the state and open the way to a new coalition with radical aims. It is in this power vacuum—what social movement theorists now call the political opportunity structure—that social movements are successfully mobilized. Often they do so in the name of grievances from the bottom, but typically such radical movements are led by upper-middle-class fractions with the best networks and organizing resources. As de Tocqueville recognized long ago, the radicalism of a movement is not correlated with the degree of immiseration; exactly what does determine the degree of radicalism is more in the realm of the ideological and emotional dynamics of exploding conflict, although just how to theorize this remains unfinished.

Virtually all revolutions, up to this point in history, have come not from economic crisis of capitalist markets, but from government breakdown. The key component is fiscal crisis in the government budget itself, but this is usually independent of major crisis in the larger economy. This means revolutions can continue to happen in the future, through the narrower mechanism of state breakdown, the state-centered fiscal crisis, elite deadlock, and ensuing paralysis of state enforcement apparatus. State crises are more frequent than full-scale economic crises. What happens when we put this in the context of the long-term trend to technological displacement of the labor force? Several things are possible: revolutions can happen in particular states, not necessarily those with the greatest amount of technological displacement. Or, revolutions can happen that do not act on a policy of solving technological displacement. But also, revolutions can happen which do take an explicitly anticapitalist turn.

Since history is driven by multiple causes, the future is like rolling multiple dice, as in the Chinese game Yahtzee—waiting for sixes to come up on all five dice simultaneously. Thus we could have the general anticapitalist revolution sometime in the future, through the right combination of state breakdown, perhaps plus war defeat, plus the omnipresent technological displacement.

The crisis of capitalism sets the agenda. At some point the politically mobilized populace will have to deal with it. This could happen by the classic route of state breakdown: the legitimacy of the state is called into question; the state itself stops functioning (paralyzed by fiscal crisis and/or political splits within its own ranks, mirroring political polarization outside); the monopoly over organized violence breaks apart, as police and the military lose organizational coherence and factionalize. This may or may not produce extensive violence, whether in riots and crowd suppression, or in civil war. In some moments of revolution (for instance the French Revolution of February 1848) the period of tense crisis was resolved with relatively little violence, as the existing regime lost organizational coherence, no one wanted to take charge of continuing the existing regime, and a new parliamentary power was quickly constituted. Similarly in Russia in February 1917, after several days of sporadic violence and wavering between crowds and soldiers, the Czarist regime ended in a flurry of abdications and refusals to pick up the reins. These cases also show that in ensuing months and years the new revolutionary regime may have trouble consolidating power, especially when restorationist movements mobilize against it, and later violence is often more severe than the initial revolutionary transition. Separating the revolutionary moment from its aftermath, the process of revolutionary state breakdown need not be very violent. Political sociology has not yet taken up the issue of under what conditions postrevolutionary consolidation of government is peaceful or violent. All we can say is that the range of violence seen in historical revolutions and their consolidation would also be possible in the terminal crisis of capitalism. The most dangerous possibility is that the prospect of anticapitalist revolution, seen by its enemies as the threat of violent change, would give rise to a neofascist solution: an authoritarian regime supported by popular movements nostalgic to save capitalism, which would carry out enough redistribution so that the massively unemployed population would be kept alive, but under a police state constantly on the alert for subversion. We do not know how to estimate the chances of an attempted fascist solution, compared to a democratic postcapitalism. Wallerstein has conjectured that it may be 50–50.

But a favorable alternative may be quite likely: the institutional transformation from capitalism to a noncapitalist system of political economy—an institutional revolution—could come about through peaceful political process. If the crisis of capitalism is severe enough—a majority of the population structurally unemployed, robots and computers doing almost all the income-generating work but owned by a small number of wealthy capitalists, the economy in deep depression—at some point a political party could win electoral power on an anticapitalist program. Some governing party or coalition would have to replace capitalist production, distribution, and finances with a system that redistributes wealth outside the system of labor market and profit-taking.

This kind of electoral politics might seem far-fetched in the political atmosphere on the present—just twenty years after the fall of the Soviet bloc, coinciding with an enormous market expansion in nominally communist China and with the triumph of market ideologies everywhere. But political moods are prone to wide swings every twenty or thirty years: think back through each twenty-year segment of the 20th century. If the structural trend to technological displacement continues to deepen, a vast reversal of opinion another twenty years into the future is not at all unlikely.

A peaceful institutional revolution is possible. The deeper the structural crisis of the middle class, the more mobilization for electoral politics is facilitated. Along that route lies the prospect for a relatively nonviolent transition.

COMPLEXITIES OF HOW STRUCTURAL CRISIS WILL UNFOLD

The world is the product of multiple intersecting causalities. Everything is clothed in particularities of locality, sequence, and memory. Thus the structural crisis of capitalism will have many variations. What is at issue here are not the names, dates, and dramas, but the big dimensions of complication—major processes that can drastically change the nature of the crisis as capitalism becomes too self-destructive to continue.

A host of processes and problems will complicate the future: aging populations, explosion of medical costs, ethnic and religious conflict, ecological crisis, huge intercontinental migrations, perhaps wars of varying scope. To keep the focus on the central point: how will these affect the technological displacement crisis? Some of them will exacerbate it; some will add pressures for state breakdown and thus raise the chances of revolutions, the rolling of multiple sixes on the dice. Will any of these complications turn back technological displacement, increasing middle class employment, creating new jobs to offset automation and computerization, and in sufficient degree that capitalism will be saved? Let us consider a brief checklist of complications, with these questions in mind.

Global unevenness. The mechanisms driving capitalist crisis operate with different intensity in different countries and regions of the world. An advanced crisis of technological displacement of middle-class work in the United States or in western Europe would not necessarily coincide with the depth of such crisis in other parts of the globe—China, India, Brazil, or other places of significance in future decades. Is it possible to have a successful anticapitalist transformation inside particular states while the rest of the world remains capitalist? This would depend on the size and weight of that particular state's economy in the world; revolutions in small states with minor economies would have little influence and might easily be overturned; those in big states with a large proportion of the world-economy would be more robust and trend-setting. Given the tendency for militarily strong regimes to intervene in other regimes, to protect their own economic interests, and to support their ideological cousins, the staggered sequence of anticapitalist regime changes could lead to interventions of the sort we have seen in the aftermath of the 2011 Arab Spring. If there were a massive economic crisis in the United States, for instance, or the EU, in the year 2030, resulting in a shift to an anticapitalist regime, possibly some other still-thriving capitalist state (China, perhaps) would intervene to stop it. Whether such interventions are successful or not will depend on geopolitical factors of relative resources, logistical extension, and geographical position [Collins 1995].

Weighing against such scenarios is a larger process: the structural crisis of capitalism is a universal tendency. Even if local hitches occur, the advance of computerization and displacement of all kinds of work will continue everywhere. No one can remain the capitalist hegemon under these conditions for long. Postcapitalist regimes, with better redistribution, may be able to generate consumer demand and get their economies back into a growth mode, pulling ahead of recalcitrant capitalist states who will be stuck in their own crises.

Muddying capitalist crisis with other dimensions of contention. In a multidimensional world, many different conflicts go on at the same time. The future showdown of capitalist crisis will be mixed with other issues; and these often have emotional and dramatic qualities that put them in the forefront of public attention.

To mention only a few: *Religion*—at present, contention most vehemently between militant Islamists and their opponents (Christians; Hindus; secularists of the post-Christian West; the post-Communist successor states, etc.); not ruling out the possibility of other axes of religious conflict in the future. *Race/ethnicity/national identity*—conflicts ranging among struggles over distribution of the spoils of office, quotas and government regulation of ethnic access to resources (affirmative action, etc.), policing borders against immigration, exclusion of immigrants, territorial disputes, and ethnic wars. But also movements to promote interethnic harmony or integration, which may be opposed in turn by movements seeking the particularistic ends listed in the previous sentence. There are also a host of transient issues that take up most of the political attention space most of the time. These involve scandals, corruption charges, personalities, atrocities, moralistic issues sometimes elevated to the status of "culture wars." But what makes structural crises more important is that they are indeed structural; they concern inescapable conflicts in the institutional arrangements that affect the material and organizational basis of ongoing social life. Unlike scandals, structural issues do not blow over; they can be ignored for a while but they continue to produce their effects.

Overlaying by particularistic issues is inevitable. Conflicts over ethnicity, religion, gender, lifestyle, etc., can either reinforce the capitalist crisis, or muddy it enough to retard or prevent a revolutionary transformation to postcapitalism. Such conflicts could also reinforce the crisis and the transformation, if large numbers of people are mobilized via their identities as suppressed and injured ethnic groups, religions, gender, etc., and perceive their grievances as coinciding with their interests in opposing the capitalist system. Overlay of particularistic identities upon class mobilization has often happened in past revolutions, and seems likely in the future. On the other hand, the overlaying most of the time diverts attention from economic issues, and has often served as the mobilizing base for reactionary movements, opposing reform of the system because of ethnic, religious, or other hostilities to the reformers. Again we should invoke the depth of the future capitalist crisis. If it is as deep as the theory indicates, there will be no way out of it, except a postcapitalist transition. All the ethnic, religious, lifestyle, and other conflicts will only be so much noise, stringing along the crisis until finally an alignment of mobilized political forces comes about that solves the problem by postcapitalist transition. The long-term result is not whether the transition will occur, but how long it will take.

War. The capitalist crisis envisioned for the mid-21st century might well be connected with wars. Anticapitalist revolution in one state could lead to subsequent wars, as the result of outside intervention to restore a procapitalist regime; or internal civil war exacerbated and sustained by outside aid and intervention; or by another path, an aggressive post-revolutionary state promoting export of revolution, thereby generating wars elsewhere. This is not inevitable; there are pathways by which a revolution (particularly a peaceful political transition) would not be followed by wars. Rather than trying to predict the contingent variety of the future, let us ask the overarching question: would wars save capitalism, or add to its crisis? Wars on the whole promote revolutions, especially on the losing side; but also sometimes on the winning side, through war expense contributing to fiscal crisis of the state. Would a war victory by a state attempting to uphold capitalism, in a world where anticapitalist movements are strong, be able to sustain capitalism by force? It might be able to do so for a period of time. But a deep crisis of massive technological displacement of work could not be solved in this way. Even this war scenario only retards the postcapitalist transformation.

Ecological crisis. Long-term climate change, destruction of natural resources and other results of human activity are producing massive consequences and endangering life and livelihood in the future. The question is: will the ecological crisis generate shifts in capitalism, such that the capitalist crisis will be overcome (the solution to the ecological crisis solving the capitalist crisis)? Or will the crises combine, making each other worse, and thereby motivating a joint solution, or a joint failure of solution?

Ecological crisis could mesh with capitalist crisis; the other prong of the alternatives, that ecological crisis would help capitalism survive, seems remote. Green industries will not generate enough employment to offset technological displacement, especially since green industries are likely to take the high-tech path of further computerization and automation. The disastrous effects of ecological crisis, although horrific to contemplate in terms of human suffering, would hit some regions of the world earlier than others. Ecological change will create new advantages and opportunities for some regions. Some low-lying parts of the world will be inundated. Other places will become relatively uninhabitable, because of drought, heat, pollution, etc. At the same time, some cold regions will become more habitable; melting ice caps will open new oceans, for instance, favoring Russia, Canada, and other regimes adjacent to these frontiers. The combination will bring about massive pressures for migration. There also could be huge population losses, amounting to a humanitarian disaster, perhaps killing hundreds of millions of people. Nevertheless, the cold eye of history centuries from now will report that even if 10% of world population were lost (or some such figure), much of the human world did survive and adjust.

Now bring the ecological crisis into juxtaposition with the crisis of capitalism generated by high-tech displacement of middle-class work. The massive flux of refugees from the ecologically devastated areas into the habitable regions would add more competition to an already crowded labor market. Cheap, expendable labor, which already drives down the life-chances of the majority made superfluous by automation, would further exacerbate the economic crisis. Some new employment would open up, in migrant ethnic enclaves, and on the geographical frontiers where the earth will become more habitable. But ecological crisis seems unlikely to break the overall trend of the technological displacement crisis. Displaced populations, fleeing from places no longer inhabitable, and the antimigrant movements that would likely follow, might add a further muddying or retarding effect on the solution of capitalist crisis. On the humanitarian side of the scale, compassion within the part of the world that welcomed such survivors could further channel emotional energy to the movement for a transition beyond capitalism and its problems. On the whole, ecological crisis seems likely to further enhance the likelihood of the anticapitalist scenario.

Of crucial importance is timing. The most careful predictions about the ecological crisis suggest that major destruction of human habitat would occur around AD 2100. It is at this point that sea levels will rise enough to inundate low-lying coastal areas; agriculture will be ruined in major populated regions; water shortages will become dire. But projections for full-scale capitalist crisis come sooner: around AD 2030–2050. The capitalist crisis will have priority, because it will hit crisis proportions first.

THE POSTCAPITALIST FUTURE AND POSSIBLE OSCILLATIONS AMONG ECONOMIC REGIMES

What comes after capitalism would have to redistribute massively from current arrangements of the private holding of wealth generated by capitalist enterprises and financial maneuverings; such redistribution would go to the large majority of the population displaced by the computerization and mechanism of all forms of labor, including much of what is now managerial and professional employment. The program of redistribution would also be the occasion to take control of what are now the financial institutions underpinning the disastrous trajectory of capitalism. Perhaps such postcapitalist institutions could be constituted in a more decentralized form than the classic 20th century experiments with state socialism.

Will the end of capitalism be the end of history? Certainly not. It will not eliminate politics. Hopefully postcapitalist regimes will be democratic; certainly there will be stronger efforts this time around, recognizing that democracy is not simply a bulwark of capitalism, but has value in itself. And politics always has the potential for new changes of direction.

Will the anticapitalist revolution make people happy? Durkheim [1893] argued that the level of happiness in human history is always about the same (perhaps we should say the level of unhappiness); new situations create new desires and new levels of comparison. In any case, conflict is intrinsic to human organization. One thing we have learned from the history of socialist regimes in the 20th century is that they have their own struggles, and that we should not expect too much from them. Chiefly they have the merit of not being capitalist, the merit of escaping from capitalist crisis.

I would not even predict that anticapitalist regimes would be permanent. Quite possibly they themselves will change, either through electoral shifts, or future revolutions another fifty to one-hundred years down the road. There is no deep reason why socialist regimes should be more peaceful than capitalist ones. As Max Weber argued, all organizations of state power strive for power prestige, when opportunities in the world-arena exist; and the military-expense path to revolution can be repeated again—in fact it was what brought down the U.S.S.R. [Collins 1995]. Far from being the end of history, future centuries may see a series of oscillations between capitalist and socialist forms, and perhaps others not yet envisioned.

It has been argued that the experience of state socialist regimes has been too unpleasant, not to say disastrous, for them to become attractive again. That has to be put in balance with the potential horrendousness of a future capitalism where a tiny elite owns all the big businesses and sells or operates all the computer equipment and the robots, leaving the great bulk of the population to scrap among themselves for jobs servicing the elite and their machines. I am not predicting the revival of utopian socialism with its grandiose hopes, but only a phase when political actors, recognizing the flaws of the alternatives, choose the escape route when one system becomes too crisis-ridden to bear. When capitalism gets bad enough, there will be turns to socialism. When state socialism has cleared up the problems for a while, its own onerous characteristics may well give rise to a reaction. Hence oscillations between the two kinds of systems of political economy, over future centuries.

Postcapitalism likely will not end all economic inequality. Past experience with socialist regimes shows they have cut the level of inequality by about one-half—compare Gini coefficients of socialist and capitalist societies, and the drastic increase in inequality following the downfall of the U.S.S.R. After socialism does something to fix the rampant inequality generated by capitalism, and to restore decent terms of employment to the majority, people may well become bored and disgruntled. Another fifty years down the line, there could be a repeat of the disenchantment with communism that took place in the 1980s. The centralized planned economy of the future may or may not be authoritarian; certainly it would have all the computerized technology, the robots, and means of coordination and surveillance to produce a heavy-handed social presence, even in its more benevolent forms. Power politics inside this kind of system will not go away, and that is another pathway toward future contention.

In addition to disgruntlement with future socialism, there would likely be rebirths of the market. If spaces are allowed inside a planned economy (and presumably in liberal, mixed forms there would be), trading networks would grow up, entrepreneurs would generate new enterprises, perhaps trumping centralized planning with their greater innovativeness. The snake in the garden, investment and finance, could make its reappearance, setting off new rounds of speculation and pyramiding meta-structures of financial manipulation. If socialist regimes are sufficiently democratic, capitalist movements might vote themselves back into office, and dismantle part or all of state direction of the economy. If the regimes are more authoritarian, the theory of revolution is back in play, waiting for circumstances that bring about state breakdown and openings for regime change. If in the distant future—for instance, the 22nd century, or the next—capitalism is restored, that too is not the end of history. If it is restored with the same tendencies to self-destruction as current capitalism, the world would see yet another repetition of swings between capitalist and anticapitalist arrangements of the economy.

In sum, the long-range future—however many centuries forward one can imagine—is likely to be a series of swings between the respective weaknesses of centralized state planning and rampant market economies. We are most certainly not looking at the emancipation of humanity, either way, but at a realistic oscillation between the horns of a socioeconomic dilemma.

CONCLUSION

I want to underline the schematic nature of my analysis. I have concentrated on a long-term structural trend in capitalist labor markets, which is at the crux of the growing inequality inside capitalism. The ongoing phase of high-tech innovation—computerization, robotization, the replacement of human communicative labor with machines—is in full swing today, and will surely become much more extreme with each passing decade. Fully advanced Artificial Intelligence does not yet exist that would closely mimic human capacities for flexible and creative cognition. The nearer AI gets to that standard, the higher the ranks of the workforce it will be able to replace. One can envision a future, perhaps less than fifty years from now, when almost all work is done by computers and robots, with a few human technicians and repair personnel. Robots are the equivalent of working-class manual labor, and factory robots have already contributed to displacing the bulk of decently paying manufacturing jobs. More advanced robots, with capacity for mobility and equipped with sensors and onboard computers, could develop into humanoid robots that would take over upper-working-class and middle-class skilled work, and then displace managers and expert professionals as well. This will not resemble the thrilling fantasies of science fiction. The real threat of the future is not some Frankensteinian revolt of the robots, but the last stage of technological displacement of labor on behalf of a tiny capitalist class of robot-owners.

Whatever the details of the technologized future turn out to be, the structural trend—the technological displacement of labor—pushes toward capitalist crisis, over and above whatever short-term, cyclical or contingent crises occur. This tendency toward increasing inequality also will undercut consumer markets, and thus eventually make capitalism unsustainable. Schematically the only way to solve the crisis will be to replace capitalism with a noncapitalist system, which means socialist ownership and strong central regulation and planning. How and where the transition will occur is much more historically singular and complicated than my theoretical scheme.

The bottom line remains: technological displacement of the middle class will bring the downfall of capitalism, in places where it is now dominant, before the 21st century is over. Whether these transitions will be peaceful or horrific remains to be seen.

References

Arrighi, Giovanni. *The Long Twentieth Century*. London: Verso, 1994.
Autor, David, and David Dorn. "The Growth of Low-Skill Service Jobs and the Polarization of the U.S. Labour Market ." *American Economic Review* 103 (2013): 1553–97. http://econ-www.mit.edu/files/1474
Brown, David K., and David B. Bills, eds. "Special Issue: New Directions in Educational Credentialism." *Research in Social Stratification and Mobility* 29 (2011): 1–138.
Chaffee, John W. *The Thorny Gates of Learning in Sung China*. Cambridge: Cambridge University Press, 1985.
Chase-Dunn, Christopher. *Global Formation. Structures of the World Economy*. Oxford: Blackwell, 1989.
Cohen, Albert K. *Delinquent Boys: the Culture of the Gang*. New York: Free Press, 1955.

Collins, Randall. *The Credential Society: An Historical Sociology of Education and Stratification.* New York: Academic Press, 1979.

Collins, Randall. "Prediction in Macro–sociology: The Case of the Soviet Collapse." *American Journal of Sociology* 100 (1995): 1552–93.

Collins, Randall. "Credential Inflation and the Future of Universities." In *The Future of the City of Intellect,* edited by Steve Brint. Stanford. CA: Stanford University Press, 2002: 100–122.

Durkheim, Emile. *The Division of Labour in Society.* New York: Free Press, 1964 (originally published 1893).

Goldstone, Jack A. *Revolution and Rebellion in the Early Modern World.* Berkeley: University of California Press, 1991.

Halnon, Karen Bettez, and Saundra Cohen. "Muscles, Motorcycles and Tattoos: Gentrification in a New Frontier." *Journal of Consumer Culture* 6 (2006): 33–56.

Milner, Murray Jr. *Freaks, Geeks and Cool Kids: American Teenagers, Schools and the Culture of Consumption.* New York: Routledge, 2004.

Schneider, Eric C. *Vampires, Dragons and Egyptian Kings. Youth Gangs in Postwar New York.* Princeton: Princeton University Press, 1999.

Schumpeter, Joseph A. *The Theory of Economic Development.* New York: Oxford University Press, 1911.

Schumpeter, Joseph A. *Business Cycles: A Theoretical, Historical, and Statistical Analysis of the Capitalist Process.* New York: McGraw-Hill, 1939.

Skocpol, Theda. *States and Social Revolutions.* New York: Cambridge University Press, 1979

Tilly, Charles. *Popular Contention in Great Britain, 1758–1834.* Cambridge MA: Harvard University Press, 1995.

Wallerstein, Immanuel. 1974–2011. *The Modern World-System.* Vols. 1–4. Berkeley: University of California Press.

White, Harrison C. *Markets from Networks.* Princeton, NJ: Princeton University Press, 2002.

Zelizer, Viviana. *The Social Meaning of Money.* New York: Basic Books, 1994.

3

THE END MAY BE NIGH, BUT FOR WHOM?

Michael Mann

INTRODUCTION

Historical sociologists like myself are good at predicting the past, but the future is another matter. It is especially difficult to predict the future of major social institutions like the nation-state or capitalism. It becomes easier if one believes that the institution in question is a "system" with its own internal logic of development, its own cycles, its own contradictions. Then we could identify the current logic of development and project a likely future. Many do believe this is possible in the case of capitalism. Neoclassical economists believe that capitalism involves regular business cycles with an inherent tendency to move toward equilibrium. So after the present difficulties of capitalism, there will come recovery, then another crisis followed by another recovery, all probably on an overall upward trajectory of development. Those who perceive deeper, less frequent but more threatening cycles, like Kondratieff or Schumpeter, have also seen them as having some internal regularity and (in the case of Kondratieff) predictability.

Even Keynes, who regarded the concept of equilibrium with some skepticism, did not deny that in the long run it would be reestablished, though with a little help from the state. These models tend to convey the image of capitalism as eternal (though not Schumpeter). Marxists also see capitalism as having an inner logic of development, but they see it—as they see all modes of production—as possessing systemic contradictions which will eventually bring it down.

The systemic element is explicit in what is called world-systems theory, whose major theorist is Immanuel Wallerstein. The only difficult part of prediction for such Marxists and systems theorists lies in the question of what will succeed it (for many of them have lost their confidence that the future is socialist). Since most intellectuals pontificating about capitalism come from the West, and since Western capitalism is obviously experiencing contemporary difficulties, doom scenarios for capitalism are currently increasing in popularity.

I wish I could share these confident visions of the future, whether optimistic or pessimistic. There are three reasons why I cannot. First, the main obstacle is my general model of human society. I do not conceive of societies as systems but as multiple, overlapping networks of interaction, of which four networks—ideological, economic, military and political power relations—are the most important. Geopolitical relations can be added to the four as a distinctive mix of military and political power, the mix varying between what are conventionally called "hard" and "soft" geopolitics. Each of these four or five sources of power may have an internal logic or tendency of development, so that it might be possible, for example, to identify tendencies toward equilibrium, cycles, or contradictions within capitalism, just as one might identify comparable tendencies within the other sources of social power. Take, for example, the cycles of attack versus defense, or mobility versus solidity, or the continuous escalation of firepower, all of which are internal tendencies of military power relations; or the long-term growth of the modern state, or the replacement of empires by nation-states, which are predominantly tendencies internal to political power relations. Ideologies, however, have distinct cycles of development, according to whether a dominant ideology seems to "work" or not, and which of the alternative ideologies currently on offer as a solution to crisis is adopted.

These different dynamics are "orthogonal" to one another. That is to say, they interact but not in a systematic way. This means that we can only identify up to a certain degree "internal" dynamics within a power source, since each is not absolutely autonomous from the others, and the development of each affects the development of the others. Once we admit the importance of such interactions we are into a more complex and uncertain world in which the development of capitalism, for example, is also influenced by ideologies, wars and states. I will demonstrate this when I seek to explain two previous crises of capitalism, the Great Depression and the present Great Recession. Unfortunately, it makes predicting the future much more difficult.

Second, complexity is heightened by the fact that planet Earth is a very big place, in which nation-states and macro-regions differ considerably from each other, so that the general tendencies just identified affect some countries and regions more than others. There might now be a really serious capitalist crisis in Greece, but only a slight one in neighboring Turkey, and almost none in China. These differences might also generate different trajectories of world-historical development, indicating for example that China might be economically overtaking the United States, or Asia the West. Macro-regional shifts have many historical predecessors.

Yet the emergence of nuclear weaponry ensures for the first time in the history of the world that any rivalry between them is unlikely to be resolved by war. But not impossible—and this raises the third complexity. Human beings are not rational calculating machines. Sometimes they face complex problems to which there is no obvious solution. Sometimes they are driven not by instrumental rationality but by what Weber called value rationality, sacrificing personal calculative interest to an overall ideology. Sometimes they are driven by strong emotions overpowering reason. So human actions are often unpredictable. In the 20th century humans often took decisions which seem to us today to have been irrational—going into two devastating world wars or seeking an utopian total transformation of human society. There is no reason to think that the twenty-first century might be different.

Thus the best I can do in the way of prediction is to pose possible alternative scenarios. I will consider whether the end or, less dramatically, the decline of capitalism might be nigh for America, for the West, for the whole global economy, or for the whole planet Earth. Some of my scenarios will be more optimistic than others, some will have more coverage of the earth than others, with the likelihood of each being affected by capitalism's complex interactions with other sources of power and other crises. I will try to assign some degree of probability to these scenarios, though these are really only rough guesses.

SYSTEMS AND CYCLES

I am skeptical of theories which depict a terminal crisis of capitalism as a single system (with two possible exceptions to be explained later). Take, for example, Wallerstein's notion that the "capitalist world-system" is in crisis. His system has two parts. The first is the "internal" crisis of capitalism, given by the logic of capital accumulation and expressed in terms of worsening Kondratieff 50–60 year cycles of boom and slump. The next slump, he says, will be much worse and may indeed finish off capitalism (he hopes so, anyway). We are now entering a systemic crisis of capitalism, he says, because profit levels are falling and they will almost inevitably keep on falling.

The second part is a geopolitical crisis manifested in longer-term "hegemonic cycles." Hegemony means domination. Crises come in the transition period between different hegemonic regimes. His examples are the transition from the hegemony of the Dutch Republic to that of the British Empire, and again from British to American hegemony. These geopolitical cycles tend to be of more variable length than the economic cycles. From the Netherlands to Britain spanned just over one hundred years, from Britain to the United States took fifty. American hegemony is now declining and will be soon ended, he says, after a reign of about seventy to eighty years. He is understandably unsure of what is to follow. He does posit Chinese hegemony as one possible future, but he seems to think it more likely that there will be no single hegemon. Given his Hobbesian view of the human need for a single Sovereign, that bodes ill. He does not see the two crises of capitalism and hegemony as undercutting or complicating each other. Instead at certain junctures crises of both the capitalist and the hegemonic cycles coincide and reinforce one another to produce a systemic crisis of the whole.

This is a succinct theory, full of insights, but I have difficulty in accepting either half of it. First, consider his list of historical hegemons. The Dutch Republic seems a bizarre choice as Europe's first hegemon. In the late 17th century the Dutch pioneered some capitalist institutions, they defended themselves well on both land and sea, and they acquired a few colonies. But they never dominated Europe, let alone the rest of the world. The Habsburgs and France were the leading powers at this time in Europe, but the continent (and its empires) had essentially multipower geopolitics. Britain was more dominant in the 19th century, for it was the leading industrial capitalist power with the biggest navy, the biggest empire, and for a time the reserve currency, but it was never hegemonic over the continent of Europe and it relied on a balance of power between other states to protect itself. Wallerstein then sees a period of rivalry between two potential hegemons, Germany and the United States, before the latter triumphed. He describes the period 1914 to 1945 as a "thirty years war" between the two, an odd description for wars into which America only entered tardily, and only when attacked by Japan in the second war. American hegemony was indeed established after World War II, but mostly as the unintended consequence of a war started by the suicidal fascist and military bravado of Germany and Japan, though these did succeed in finishing off the British and French Empires. US hegemony over much of the world was completed by the Soviet Union turning inwards into economic autarchy. Such a contingent set of outcomes resulted from complex interactions among all four sources of social power. The United States was already in the interwar period the leading economic power—though without World War II the dollar would have probably shared reserve status with other national currencies—but had much less military or geopolitical power. The outcome of the war was that America became the great historical exception, the only global empire, the only true hegemon the world has ever seen. But with only a single case, it is hard to identify hegemonic cycles. Nonetheless, I do agree with Wallerstein that the United States has been hegemonic in the recent past, that its hegemony is now weakening, and that it may well end sometime around 2020 to 2025. This unique world-historical process may lead to a crisis specific to the United States.

What about the supposed Kondratieff cycles, successive waves of upswings and downswings of almost fixed duration? Kondratieff suggested that his K-waves lasted 54 years. If so, since the economy hit rock bottom in 1933, it should have risen for 27 years until 1960 and then declined until another low point of 1987, and then boomed to peak in 2014. It doesn't feel like an upswing today! Those following in his footsteps have dated cycles in two different ways according to whether they are measuring swings in prices or production volumes. Some see 1972–1973 as the beginning of an upswing (since prices rose), others the beginning of a downswing (actually production did not fall but its rate of growth slowed—at least in the West). The two world wars produced further disagreements: did an upswing end in 1913 or 1929, and did another upswing begin in 1938 or 1945? There is little agreement about such cycles, which makes us doubt their regularity.

Wallerstein has his own version of K-waves. He says the last upswing (in production) began in 1945 and peaked in 1967–1973. That seems true of the Western part of the economy, but this was less the product of a cycle internal to capitalism than of the end of World War II, which had provided an extraneous economic stimulus. A globally regulated capitalism agreed upon initially by Britain and the United States and then agreed to by all US allies was established, and it could thrive on pent-up consumer demand, forcibly restrained during the war, combining with wartime technological improvements to generate an unprecedented "golden age," with growth greater than ever seen before and spreading across almost the whole world. Following this period the economy in the West remained fairly stagnant from about 1973 until 2000, when the upswing should have begun. It hasn't yet, a decade later. But note that for large parts of the world the boom continued after the West faltered and is still continuing for some countries. First Japan, then East Asian countries and China, then India, then the other BRICs have all experienced booms. K-waves are controversial even among economists studying the West, but for much of the Rest they seem irrelevant.

Upswings and downswings are inevitable in capitalism and it may be that after a long up-swing actors become overconfident and head for a harder fall. Certainly bankers and home buyers did in the first decade of the twenty-first century. But any precise, regular patterning seems elusive, while truly global patterns are rare. Yet it may be possible that past crises might give us some kind of guide to a future crisis of capitalism. So, being a believer that theories must be based on detailed empirical study, I turn to the two most severe, best-evidenced crises in the history of capitalism, the Great Depression and the present Great Recession.[1]

THE GREAT DEPRESSION

Both crises had multiple causes. Most of these were predominantly internal economic causes, as we might expect since these were economic events and capitalism does have a degree of "internal" logic. But some causes came from

---

[1] I discuss them much more intensively in the last two volumes of my *The Sources of Social Power*: The Great Depression in Volume 3, Chapter 7, and Volume 4, Chapter 11: *Global Empires and Revolution, 1890–1945*. (New York: Cambridge University Press, 2012), and the Great Recession in Volume 4: *Globalizations, 1945–2012* (New York: Cambridge University Press, 2013.)

outside the economy, and some were rather contingent. In both cases crisis began with one serious problem which then turned by stages into something greater as it "found out" and exacerbated other weaknesses, hitherto overlooked, some economic, some not. The whole process might easily have gone otherwise. It also hit unevenly across the world, leaving some national economies virtually unscathed, while some countries escaped quite quickly through effective policies. All these are reasons for doubting that there is a single systemic logic at work. Unfortunately they also lessen the chances of predicting economic crises in the future.

The Great Depression began with overproduction in agriculture (partly due to World War I) and was then racheted upward by a gold standard no longer maintained (as in the prewar period) neither by cooperation between the central banks of the Great Powers nor by British hegemony, as Barry Eichengreen has shown. Individual countries returned after the war to the gold standard in an ad hoc way, mostly at unrealistic levels driven by ideologies of national pride and honor more than by pragmatic economic analysis. Also contributing were geopolitical tensions between Germany and Austria, on the one hand, and France and Britain on the other. France and America hoarded gold. There was ideological attachment by old regimes to laissez-faire economics, a stock market bubble, and an uncompleted transition from old to new forms of manufacturing, all of which lowered the employment potential of the economy. In America, the eye of the storm, grave policy mistakes were also made by Congress and by the Federal Reserve Board rooted in the market fundamentalism of this period which reached its ghastly climax in what was called "liquidationism"–the pursuit of austerity measures in order to destroy inefficient firms, industries, investors, and workers. Absent any two or three of these varied causes cascading on top of each other and we would have been labeling this a cyclical recession. But the cascade was by no means inevitable.

The Depression is often treated as being global but it struck unevenly. It struck Western Europe and the Anglophone countries hard, though even in these zones the United States, Canada, and Germany lost six times as much per capita income as Britain did, and three times as much as France did. But after the first dip the Depression barely affected large swaths of the world. China was only slightly affected, while the Soviet Union, Japan, its colonies Korea and Taiwan, and Eastern Europe continued to grow through the Depression. So the Depression was in reality less than global. Perhaps we should really label it the Great White Depression, for the white race was the worst affected. Some countries then got out of the Depression relatively quickly by leaving the gold standard and reflating their economies. The United States eventually did this, but the Roosevelt administration's overconfidence that recovery was underway led it to deflate in 1937, which produced a "double-dip" recession. In fact, only the enhanced industrial demand of World War II enabled a full recovery in the United States.

It is obvious from all this that noneconomic causes were quite important. As an example, I pick out the role of military power relations in the crisis. World War I had significant influences on the Depression. During the war many poorer countries had been able to greatly increase their agricultural exports. When agriculture in the combatant countries came back onstream after the war, this generated overproduction and so there were serious price falls. But the war had also destroyed the consensual gold standard, and the failure of the peace treaties to solve geopolitical rivalries made international cooperation over political economy more difficult. Crisis was not the necessary outcome of multipower geopolitics, for these had produced economic stability before the war; it was a consequence of the geopolitical legacy of a particularly terrible war.

The systemic argument could be supported if the war had been caused by either capitalism or declining British hegemony, but neither was the case. Europe had for centuries before the arrival of capitalism been an unusually warlike continent, war was still the default mode of diplomacy, and this war, like many previous wars in the continent, was started when major powers went to the defense of their minor clients (now Serbia and Belgium). Militarism was a European tradition (see my The Sources of Social Power Volume 3, Chapters 2 and 5). In the Great Depression different causal chains came together like tributaries swelling into a great river, with various mini-crises cascading into a deeper crisis as they "found out" further weaknesses; that the different shocks kept coming had not been anticipated by anyone.

THE GREAT RECESSION, 2008

The vital question here is whether the present recession will continue, worsen, and even perhaps set in motion forces which might bring down capitalism. However, let me first briefly analyze its causes. We also find a cascade pattern here. The recession began as primarily an American crisis with

several causal chains coming together. First, American hegemony and consequent global imbalances enabled the government and ordinary Americans
to borrow vast sums of money from abroad at negligible interest rates, building up debts that eventually proved unsustainable. Second, the consequent
increase in interest rates burst the mortgage bubble and this triggered the
first actual shock. However, this causal sequence also required input from
politicians' ideological commitment to creating a "property-owning democracy," a nation of home-buyers. The third main cause was that this occurred
after a demolition of financial regulation; and the fourth was grossly widening inequality in the United States. Both of these last two were inspired
by the conjunction of neoliberal ideology and bankers' and top managers'
power within the American political system. This can be partly attributed
to an American shift from manufacturing to financial services which helped
make short-term "shareholder value" the main corporate goal. Similar causes
operated in the United Kingdom, for finance capital and neoliberalism were
dominant in both countries. These causes were not so pronounced in most
other countries, though the German phobia concerning inflation (caused by
the historical myth that inflation had caused the rise of Hitler) was compatible with the policies urged by neoliberals, and German economic power
within Europe transmitted this fiscal conservatism across the continent.
Military power did not matter in the Great Recession, but ideological power
did, in the form of neoliberalism and inflation phobia.

These pressures then "found out" the whiz kids of the financial services
sector. Their mathematical equations had led to a misplaced confidence
in abstruse financial instruments with less and less relationship to the real
economy. They had converted the ideology of neoclassical economics into
mathematical models of risk, falsely believing that economies are purely
market systems all of whose principal parameters can be precisely calculated
and predicted. Almost no-one had foreseen that the various elements of risk
might cascade on top of each other.

Crisis was then diffused internationally not because American hegemony
was in decline but because America, its economy, its dollar, and its mathematical economists remained hegemonic. The decline in US economic activity then affected countries with debt problems and also countries which
were major US trading partners but which had been "virtuous," not seduced
by debts or greatly widening inequality, neoliberalism, or finance capital,
like Germany and France. Closer scrutiny by scared investors then "found

out" sectors and countries whose debts were also revealed to be unsustainable once the recession and capital contraction started. In 2007, just before the recession, IMF figures for European states show that only Greece and Italy had public debt levels slightly higher than their GDPs. The average level of government debt across the EU was slightly lower than among the OECD countries as a whole (71% to 73%). Only in Greece was the level of government debt the real problem. In Ireland, Spain and Italy (as in America and Britain) it was private debt that had rocketed—though the main weakness of the Italian economy was its low level of productivity. These economies all had different weaknesses which might not have been "found out" without the American-driven financial crisis. But when recession struck and was worsened by austerity policies, lesser economic activity meant lesser revenues, and so government debt now rocketed everywhere.

The crisis in Europe then worsened when the recession "found out" a quite extraneous weakness of the Eurozone which turned the recession into a major sovereign debt crisis, caused in the first place by the zone's own internal imbalances. There had been a big outflow of capital from the richer EU countries to the poorer ones, with the Greek government contributing its distinctive dose of fiscal dishonesty. But this crisis had only intensified because of the enthusiasm of the elites of the seventeen eurozone countries—not their peoples and not the elites of the remaining ten EU countries—for "deepening" the Union through a common currency without ensuring adequate backing of the euro by a central bank with treasury and fiscal functions. This was a structural political weakness. The elites knew they would not be able to adequately back up the euro if weaker countries the size of Italy or Spain went to the wall. But as convinced Europeanists they were willing to take this risk even though their national electorates would have rejected any proposal to create a single treasury, and they knew this because the voters had opposed a milder deepening of the EU in each of the last three national referenda held in eurozone countries. For these elites political ideals had trumped their economic sagacity to produce a terrible policy mistake. The European crisis was then worsened by the depth of the austerity programs being pushed for different ideological reasons by both Britain and Germany and forced on the weaker European economies. A contingent conjunction of different economic, ideological, and political causal chains (not military in this case) still threatens to cascade into a much worse "double-dip" recession.

Again, however, the Great Recession spread very unevenly around the world. From World Bank data on GDP growth we can see that almost every country had a difficult 2008 or 2009. In this brief phase the crisis was indeed global. It then deepened in the United States, and across Europe as far east as Russia and its eastern neighbors, and in some poor indebted countries. But by 2010 numerous countries had bounced back to achieve their highest GDP growth rates of the 21st century—including important countries like Brazil, Mexico, Turkey, Nigeria, Canada, Malaysia, Korea, and Singapore. India and Indonesia recovered to almost their previous highest levels, while China's official growth rate fell from about 10% to 8%, still the envy of the world! All these countries except for Canada are what we used to refer to as "underdeveloped" countries. Most of them had learned the lessons of the structural adjustment decades and had built up reserves to avoid large debts to foreigners. Those countries which had not acted in this way were worse affected. Canada escaped because its newer extractive industries meant a lesser role for the banking sector, which it also kept tightly regulated. That might have been enough for escape in other countries. If this became a systemic crisis, it was one that could have been evaded by different policies.

So like the Great Depression, the Great Recession was only disastrous for some countries. The American virus did spread across the world, mainly through financial channels, though the reduction of international trade mattered too. But many countries got out quickly because they had different structural arrangements, some economic, some political, some ideological. The main structures that worked were: corporatist or developmental states (South Korea); economies whose strong growth did not include a large financial sector (most of them); little neoliberalism (most of them); or merely having prudent policies like the avoidance of foreign debt (most of the Asian cases) or maintaining strict regulation of finance capital (Canada). Almost the whole of South and Southeast Asia plus Oceania, a very large macro-region, was little affected for these reasons and also because this region traded heavily with China (important for the Australian recovery). As in the Great Depression the right policies could minimize the damage, the wrong policies could worsen it. The politics and ideologies which flourish within different macro-regions matter for the outcome. Thus the sovereign debt crisis of the eurozone came as the diffusion of the American crisis interacted with different causal chains—the distinctive political rhythms and institutions of the European Union, and the ideological preference for austerity and avoidance of inflation of German (and British) elites. The internal logic of capitalism in many developing countries would intrinsically lead to further growth. If there is a threat to this it comes from outside, from the self-induced weaknesses of America and Europe.

Will the present crisis worsen and engulf almost everyone? If the eurozone collapses, that would obviously be terrible news for its countries, but it would also have a major global impact on trade and investment. It would immediately hit hard the non-eurozone European countries, like the United Kingdom, since they trade with and invest in the eurozone more than anywhere else. The hit would also reach across neighboring countries, from Russia through the Near East and North Africa, as well as to America, a major trading partner of, and investor in, Europe. South America would suffer as well, especially from a collapse in the Spanish economy. If both the EU and America experienced economic contraction then the effect on global trade would be very bad, since they provide almost half of world GDP and the level of economic globalization is now higher than ever. India and especially China would also find their exports decline significantly. That would indicate a systemic crisis of capitalism, worse than the "double-dip" recession predicted by many. Yet even so it would be probably worse in the West than among the developing Rest.

This cascade might actually happen, though the eurozone countries may be able to cobble together a financial fix, since it is the elites, not the masses, who control the EU, and by now the elites have realized that they have common interests in finding a solution, at almost whatever the cost. The problem here (as elsewhere) is that the financial resources now available to bail out or stimulate the economy are less than in 2008. I emphasize, however, that human action and political will matter considerably, which means we cannot actually predict the outcome. However, I will predict that if many more countries take the neoliberal austerity route through this recession, as proposed by American Republicans and actually implemented by the British Conservative government, and if the inflation phobia of Germans reinforces this, then another Great Depression, this time quite likely to be more globally systemic, will follow. If, however, the Europeans realize and act on their collective interests and if countries take the more Keynesian route being advocated by the French government of financing a stimulus (partly by higher taxes on those who are more able to pay), then this might prevent further worsening. In either case, recovery would probably eventually happen, though more slowly in the former case—and this time without the benefit of a world war. Whether recovery would ever restore full employment is something I will discuss later.

Capitalism is subject to cycles, though whether they have a regular patterning through time is another matter. Occasionally the recession phase of the cycle gets much worse, partly through "internal" economic causes, partly through costly wars, stalemated politics, or ideologies generating policies inappropriate to the crisis. In both major cases of Depression/Recession this was an important cause of worsening, the first time because no other plausible macroeconomic ideology had yet emerged, the second time because it came after a long period of market growth ended by the apparent failure of the Keynesian alternative, followed by deregulation, especially of the financial sector. Political and geopolitical relations matter as well, and they seem much less predictable. There do seem to be economic lessons to draw from these crises which in theory might reduce the likelihood of future crises. But it is far from clear that powerful elites have drawn the appropriate lessons. Neoliberal austerity programs inflicted on economies in recession unfortunately recall the unhelpful role of liquidationism at the beginning of the 1930s. Note also that in the 20th century the two terrible wars had absolutely contrary effects, further worsening the problem of prediction. The first war helped intensify a recession into the Great Depression, the second substantially contributed to the biggest boom of all—and to American hegemony.

AMERICAN HEGEMONY AND ITS DISCONTENTS

It is therefore possible that America will suffer the greatest economic decline in the near future. Wallerstein suggests that the period of greatest American strength was 1945–1970, after which there has been continuous decline. I am not so sure. The American share of the world's total GDP actually declined from 1950 to 1970, because of the recovery of Japan and Europe. It then remained virtually static from 1970 to 2005 as the United States successfully exploited the advantages of having the dollar as the reserve currency of the world. A relative decline has occurred since then, largely a product of the higher growth of India and China, but the dollar remains almighty, America can still borrow unlimited cash at an interest rate of lower than 2%, and in most years it still outperforms Europe and Japan in economic productivity and growth. The IMF and Barry Eichengreen have both guessed that the dollar will remain as the world's reserve currency until some date soon after 2020. The United States also has 48% of the world's military expenditure, its highest-ever percentage, and it retains its dominance over patents, Nobel prizes, elite universities, and popular culture. America remains hegemonic, for better or for worse.

It will not last, of course, and there are suspicions that premonitions of decline are just beginning to haunt Americans. Its gigantic military has experienced what are in effect defeats over the last decade. Its political and ideological power relations have reached near-crisis level. Rising divisive inequality has been deliberately encouraged by politicians. The merging of top management and big corporate investors (especially the bosses of insurance and pension funds) so that they are essentially paying themselves exorbitant salaries and bonuses (on which they only have to pay 15% rather than 35% tax rates) also grossly widens inequality. The combination of regressive taxes, corporate plundering, and anemic economic growth has led to economic recession and to ideological alienation.

But American alienation is not currently leading toward a political solution, since it has generated two opposed notions of what should be done. One, led by the Republican Party, blames government for the economic ills of the country and proposes to reduce its size, its regulatory powers, and its taxes in order to restore a market-driven prosperity. Its preference for austerity measures as a way out of recession makes it uncomfortably close to the "liquidationist" strategy which deepened the Great Depression. The other solution, proposed by liberal Democrats, blames big corporations and banks, symbolically labeled as "Wall Street," and proposes more government regulation, more redistributive taxes, and a more state-sponsored Keynesian path to growth through increased public expenditures. The current political stalemate and especially the deeply reactionary, backward-looking stances of the Republican Party do not augur well for America's ability to meet these enormous future challenges. America suffers from anomie, an absence of shared norms, as well as alienation—Durkheim as well as Marx. (as Durkheim argued, anomie lessens social cohesion and fosters decline).

Republicans' proposals of austerity for the masses but prosperity for the rich are seen by them as job-creating measures, but the rich do not consume much. Instead they save, producing capital surpluses and lower interest rates, encouraging the consumer debt which brought on the recession in the first place. This threatens the basis of the mass consumer demand economy on which American wealth has rested during the postwar period. Republican ideology has also turned increasingly against science, which does not bode well for the future of America. The Republicans are more united over economic policies than are the Democrats, whose main problem is internal divisions. This has allowed the Republicans to dictate recent policy agendas. Republican leaders used to be ideological in their rhetoric but pragmatic in their actual policies. But free-market fundamentalism is more resonant in American popular culture than is state interventionism. In the postwar boom period real economic policy took the form of "commercial Keynesianism," state-steered markets, a compromise between market and state. But the political rhetoric of the time, especially on the Republican side, focused almost entirely on free markets and free enterprise. Americans had actually gotten a large state, but they pretended they had not. So appealing to free markets has a political edge today because it is more ideologically rooted in America than are appeals to a beneficent state. The electorate as well as the politicians may not be able to embrace useful economic policies.

There are other American weaknesses too. There are very high military and health expenditures—both more than double those of any other country. These achieve very poor outcomes in terms of military interventions abroad and in terms of mortality and longevity statistics at home. Yet they are still regarded by politicians as being near-sacrosanct, as is the credo of no new taxes. Thus their draining of economic resources and their increasing of the public debt are likely to continue, adding further burdens on the country. These weaknesses in all four sources of social power might bring America down. We cannot know for sure. Americans remain highly inventive and hardworking. Their industries remain mostly dynamic. They might be able to put their ideological, financial, military and political houses back together again. If they don't, then when the dollar loses its reserve currency status, Americans will be less able to borrow and their military will decline unless they are willing to pay much higher taxes—which seems unlikely. US hegemony will end sooner or later in this coming half-century, and the end might not be graceful.

But that need not cause a systemic crisis of capitalism. The successor to American hegemony is unlikely to be another single hegemonic power—not China, not India, not any other individual state. Their growth rates are stratospheric now but they will inevitably decline toward more normal levels once they reach a more mature level of industrialism and postindustrialism.

They will also have crises of their own to surmount. No country will be as powerful in the future as the United States has recently been. Human society will be in uncharted waters, moving toward more multipower politics and to a coordinated basket of reserve currencies. This has been the normal state of affairs in human history and it has not served the world economy too badly. It was accompanied in the first half of the 20th century by devastating war, but there are now reasons to believe that inter-state war is a thing of the past—especially when Americans lose their enthusiasm for war.

But that list of countries who have so far escaped lightly does reinforce the sense that economic power is shifting from the old West to the successfully developing countries of the Rest of the world, including most of Asia. The likeliest scenario in the medium term is a sharing of economic power between the United States, the European Union, and the four BRICs (Brazil, Russia, India and China)–but amid world peace. Since the BRICs' economies—and especially those of Russia and China—contain more state regulation than most Western countries—and especially the United States—the capitalism of the medium term is likely to be more statist.

The Exhaustion of Capitalist Markets?

Here I shift to the long term. So far I have been skeptical of notions that capitalism has general "laws of motion" that lead regularly to systemic crises. I have depicted major crises of the past and present less as singular and systemic than as cascades of distinct causal chains, both economic and noneconomic, piling unexpectedly on top of each other, sometimes rather contingently. So far crises have also struck unevenly across the world and they have been responsive to shifts in geoeconomic and geopolitical power. Previous crises have not really signaled world-system weaknesses. Instead they have indicated geographical shifts in power within global capitalism and within global geopolitics.

But in this book neither Immanuel Wallerstein nor Randall Collins draws on previous or present crises when envisaging the possible end of capitalism across the globe. Rather they identify secular tendencies of capitalist development which they believe may doom it in the future. They argue that there are finite limits to capitalism's ability to sustain profit and employment. They firstly cite the geographic limits of planet Earth's markets. They note that capitalist growth is steadily filling up planet Earth. They also note that capitalists in the advanced countries solved the problem of low-growth phases by exporting manufacturing to places where cheaper, less-regulated labor yielded them greater profit. This is what some have called the "spatial fix" to capitalist crisis. Jobs were moved from the American North to the American South, then to Latin America, then China, then Vietnam, and the process will continue into Africa and central Asia. Collins is especially worried by what he sees as the export of middle-class intellectual labor to other countries of the world. So what happens when all these regions are absorbed and capitalist markets fill up the Earth?

Wallerstein suggests that it takes about thirty years from the entry of major investment in a rural country to get workers sufficiently organized to force wages up and capital out. So when the Earth has filled up, labor costs will be high everywhere and profits will fall. Capitalists will try nonetheless to reduce wages but they will now be dealing with a globally organized working class. It will resist, producing a global crisis of capitalism. This scenario will take a while yet. Only a part of the enormous populations of India and China have as yet been absorbed into a minimally regulated industrial or postindustrial economy. That will take more than thirty years. Moreover, the process hasn't yet begun in Africa or central Asia so that such a fill-up may take up until the end of the 21st century, especially since population growth is projected to continue until near the end of the century and it will be biggest in the poorest countries.

However, I find this model of an earth reaching the limits of economic markets difficult to understand. If there is no cheap labor left, capitalists can no longer reap superprofits from this source, but the higher productivity of labor and increased consumer demand in newly developed countries might compensate for this and produce a reformed capitalism on a global scale, with more equality and social citizenship rights for all. This would not mean the end of capitalism but rather a better capitalism in which the whole planet would enjoy the kinds of rights enjoyed by workers in the post-World War II West. After all, in that period the vast bulk of the wealth of the advanced countries was created through trade and production among themselves, not with the rest of the world (oil excluded). The boom of the postwar period came mainly as a result of a high productivity/high consumer demand economy of the advanced countries themselves. It did not mainly depend on highly exploited Southern labor. Why should this not be so in the future, but for the whole world?

Moreover, new markets need not be restricted by geography. They can also be created by cultivating new needs. Capitalism has grown adept at persuading families that they need two cars, bigger and bigger houses, more and more electronic devices. Whoever dreamt of this fifty years ago? What will our grandchildren consume fifty years from now? We cannot begin to envisage their consumer fads, but we can be sure there will be some. Markets are not fixed by territory. Planet Earth can be filled and yet new markets can be created. That, of course, depends on what some have called the "technological fix" and it is more or less what Joseph Schumpeter called "creative destruction," which he identified as being the core of capitalist dynamism—entrepreneurs pour money into technological innovation which results in the creation of new industries and the destruction of old ones. The Great Depression in the United States was partially caused by the stagnation of the major traditional industries, while the new emerging industries, though vibrant, were not yet big enough to absorb the surplus capital and labor of the period. That was achieved in World War II and the aftermath, which then suddenly released enormous consumer demand held back by wartime sacrifices.

So the vital question now is whether another technological fix is occurring or is likely to soon occur. There are new dynamic industries like microelectronics and biotechnology. But the problem is that so far they have not been big enough to provide a satisfactory fix, especially for the labor market in the West, where the new industries tend to be more capital- than labor-intensive. The decline of manufacturing industry in much of the West has generated unemployment there which the newer industries have not been able to much reduce. Recent innovations like computers, the Internet and mobile communication devices do not compare with railroads, electrification and automobiles in their ability to generate profit and employment growth. The "Green Revolution" has been the recent exception, providing a great boost to agricultural production, mainly in the poorer countries. Also important has been the expansion of the health and educational sectors, which are more labor intensive and in which the labor is more intellectual and more middle class. Their expansion is likely to continue, as the length of life, and especially of old age, and educational credentialism continue to increase.

Randall Collins is quite persuasive in his enumeration and then rejection of various possible scenarios whereby human societies might fight against the scourge of declining employment. Yet the reverse is happening right now. Economic expansion over the last few decades has actually produced a growth in global employment, greater even than the substantial rise in world population. Between 1950 and 2007 job growth was about 40% higher than population growth. In the Organization for Economic Cooperation and Development (OECD) an organization representing the richer countries of the world more people are also working than ever before, though the absolute number of unemployed has also risen because the population is larger and a higher proportion of the population seeks jobs, including far more women. The liberation of women in the formal labor market has been the biggest problem for employment in the West. But the global unemployment rate remained fairly stable between the 1970s and 2007, at around 6%. Even through the Great Recession ILO statistics collected by the International Labor Organization reveal that global employment has continued to grow, though at only half the rate before the crisis and unevenly distributed across the world. It fell in 2009 in the developed economies, including the European Union (by 2.2%) and its neighbors, and in the ex-soviet Commonwealth of Independent States (by 0.9%), but it grew in all the other regions of the world. The employment-to-population ratio also fell back in the advanced countries, and in east Asia, but elsewhere by 2010 this ratio was back to the 2007 level. Unemployment is as yet a Western (and to a lesser extent a Japanese) not a global problem.

The West's loss is the Rest's gain, and the world as a whole benefits. Yet the future of labor markets in the advanced countries may be labor shortages, not high unemployment. The length of life is still growing and the birth-rate has fallen below the level necessary to reproduce the population. Europe, Japan and North America will need substantial immigration to make up the gap. Since these demographic tendencies are likely to continue as other countries become more developed, overall world population is predicted to begin falling in the second half of the 21st century. These are reasons why mass unemployment may not eventuate and precipitate the end of capitalism.

As Collins says, there is no necessary reason why capitalism should be indefinitely capable of generating enough creation to compensate for the destruction. There has simply been a long period in which this happened. But equally, there is no necessary reason why creative destruction should end. Who knows what new needs the development process will create? I suggest one further creative sector later.

But supposing the pessimism of my colleagues is correct. This might produce one of two alternative futures which seem to me to be more likely than capitalist collapse. The first is a rather pessimistic capitalist scenario in which structural employment remains high and a "2/3–1/3" society emerges. Two-thirds are well educated, highly skilled, in regular employment, doing quite well, but with a third excluded from this society. The poor might receive enough welfare and charity to keep them from revolting, or they might be repressed. They would be a minority, so their chances of successful revolution would be small. It is a distinct possibility that the included would not sympathize much with the excluded. They might have negative views of them as worthless dropouts, scroungers, welfare queens, etc. In some countries ethnic or religious minorities would be overrepresented among the poor, and negative ethnic/religious slurs would be added to these stereotypes. The excluded might become a hereditary lower class, reinforcing the gulf between included and excluded. Most of the included would vote to maintain this gulf, while many of the excluded would not vote. The extent of welfare might continue to differ across the West, with countries like Sweden and Germany being willing to keep the poor within mainstream society, while countries like the United States might not. We can recognize this pessimistic scenario, for it is already present in the United States, and sociologists have perceived its rise in Europe too. It would be the final demise of the working class—but not of capitalism. It would produce an asymmetric class structure such as existed through most of history, now with capitalists well organized, workers divided and less organized. Social institutions survive even when they do not perform very well, unless counterorganization emerges among the oppressed.

It has not yet emerged, and this scenario is especially chilling for leftists—a more exploitative but unchallenged capitalism. Never has the global left been so weak as today. The World Social Forum, a global organization of radicals headquartered in Porto Alegre, Brazil has been a significant force in the period during which Southern protests against Northern/Western oppression were rooted in global capitalist exploitation by the West. But the "South" is developing yet also ceasing to exist as a coherent whole. This is now evident in recent climate change discussions in which China, India and Brazil have joined forces with the West and Japan to delay emissions reductions, against the objections of poorer countries.

The second alternative scenario is more optimistic. It agrees that capitalist markets will fill up the planet and that profit and growth rates will fall. But it suggests that this will stabilize into an enduringly low-growth capitalism. That would not be new, of course. Capitalism's great breakthrough came in

18th and 19th century Britain. Yet the British growth rate never exceeded 2% in any one year. The British success story was rather that an average growth of just above 1% per annum continued for a very long time. In the 20th century, however, the pace quickened. Between the wars, the most successful developing countries (Japan, its colonies, and the Soviet Union) achieved historically unprecedented growth rates of around 4%. Then in the late 20th century China and India (and now others) achieved growth rates of around 8%. Though those rates have endured for at least two decades, they will inevitably decline. Then Africa and Central Asia might do even better. But they all have a lot of time before they might be reduced down to the 1% level of the historic British success story. Maybe the American and European rates might decline more quickly to this level but in the current Great Recession only a few countries saw negative growth rates, and then only for a year or two. Why should a growth rate of 1% be a capitalist crisis? Why cannot capitalism continue as a low-growth global system, which it was for much of its history? The 20th century—more precisely, the period 1945 to 1970 in the West and the end of the 20th century in the East—would then be seen as exceptional. This low-growth scenario would also reduce the role of speculation and downgrade the power of finance capital, with repeats of our present Great Recession (which are at present quite likely) becoming less likely. Of course, as labor conditions improve throughout the world, that is very good news. Then all of humanity might live in an almost steady-state economy, like the Japanese have already done for the last twenty years. The future of capitalism might not be tumultuous, but boring.

If forced to choose one scenario as the most likely to occur sometime around 2050 (if nothing else in the meantime interfered), I would plump for a lower-growth global capitalism spreading more equality of condition across the world but carrying a casually employed or unemployed lower class of somewhere between 10% and 15% of national populations, a mixture of the two scenarios depicted above and very much like the 19th century industrializing countries. I would not predict much revolution.

There is a further obstacle to revolutionary change. The communist and fascist revolutionary alternatives to capitalism were disasters, and they are the only ones to have emerged so far. There are no other alternatives around and almost no one wants to repeat either of those. Socialism, whether revolutionary or reformist, has never been weaker. Fundamentalist Christianity, Judaism, Hinduism, and Islam are the surging ideologies of the world and they tend to contemplate otherworldly as much as material salvation. This-worldly alternative ideologies of the 20th century failed. In poorer countries brought into the global economy we might expect the rise of socialist or similar movements, but they are likely to become reformist. Modern social revolutions have almost never occurred without major wars destabilizing and delegitimizing ruling regimes. In the two biggest revolutions of the 20th century, in Russia and China, world wars (with different causes than capitalist crises) were necessary causes of revolution. Wars are thankfully in decline around the world—in fact only the United States continues to make interstate wars—and there are no anticapitalist revolutionary movements of any size in the world. Revolution seems an unlikely scenario. The end really is nigh for revolutionary socialism.

The future of the left is likely to be at most reformist social democracy or liberalism. Employers and workers will continue to struggle over the mundane injustices of capitalist employment (factory safety, wages, benefits, job security, etc.), and their likely outcome will be compromise and reform. Developing countries will likely struggle for a reformed and more egalitarian capitalism just as Westerners did in the first half of the 20th century. Some will be more successful than others, as was the case in the West. China faces the severest problems now. The benefits of its phenomenal growth are very unequally distributed, generating major protest movements. Revolutionary turbulence is certainly possible there, but if successful it would likely bring in more capitalism and perhaps an imperfect democracy, as happened in Russia. America also faces severe challenges since its economy is overloaded with military and health spending, its polity is corrupted and dysfunctional, and the ideology of its conservatives has turned against science and social science. All this amid the inevitability of relative decline and the growing realization that American claims to a moral superiority over the rest of the world are hollow. This seems a recipe for further American decline.

The End of the World?

Yet all the scenarios I have sketched so far might be thrown out of gear by two other potential crises which might be even greater than the two world wars. Both are absolutely novel and both would be truly systemic and global. These would not be confined within national or macro-regional borders since they emerge out of the atmosphere all humans breathe.

The first global threat is the military one of nuclear war. The severity of this threat is almost completely unpredictable since it depends on a whole sequence of events any one of which might not happen. So far there have only been two-power confrontations, first the United States (and its British and French allies) against the Soviets, then India against Pakistan, flanked by a rather passive China. In these cases the threat of mutually assured destruction has been obvious to the two sides and the response, after a couple of half-crises, has been disciplined avoidance of escalation. Nuclear deterrence has worked.

However, when more than two powers are involved in more complex conflicts, outcomes become more fraught. It was multipower conflicts in which some could not read the intentions of others which produced both world wars. In the Middle East Israel already has nuclear weapons, Iran is nearing that goal, and that might provoke neighboring powers to drive for them as well. That would be dangerous for the Middle East, for their neighbors, for much of the world's oil supplies, and even for the whole world. These arms races have little to do with capitalism. If nuclear war did break out, then capitalism would be seen by any survivors as having been only a minor player in the disaster. However, maybe Iran will be persuaded away from nuclear weapons; maybe Saudi Arabia, Iraq and Turkey will not retaliate by acquiring them; and maybe human reason can even surmount the dangers posed by multiple rival powers armed with nuclear weapons. Yet then there is the possible scenario of terrorists stealing a nuclear weapon. Who can predict the outcome here since some terrorists do appear to be motivated by otherworldly goals? Theirs might be the most dangerous ideology ever.

The second systemic crisis is in contrast highly predictable—unless extraordinary evasive action is taken. Climate change is happening (I deal with this in Volume 4, Chapter 12). The air, sea and land are warming while also experiencing more fluctuations in temperatures, predominantly because of human actions. The threat is global, since greenhouse gas emissions anywhere affect people everywhere. These emissions come flanked by other disaster scenarios: food and water shortages, polar icecap and tundra melting, seawater inundations, etc. Millions of people are already dying prematurely as a result of global warming and the survival of a few poorer countries will be threatened within twenty to thirty years unless human societies radically change the direction of their development.

If humanity does act in time to substantially reduce emissions, it has to radically challenge and reform the three major institutions which have achieved such success over the last century. The first one is capitalism—though only because this is now the dominant mode of production in the world. State socialism in its heyday was just as destructive of the environment. As radical environmentalists say, we have to get society off "the treadmill of profit." This might mean disciplining business through a severe regulatory "command and control" state, or through taxation levied on the throughput of resources in enterprises, or through market mechanisms like stringent "cap and trade" programs which provide incentives for capitalists to turn toward investment in virtuous low-emissions industries. If such policies are pursued rigorously, capitalism will survive, even if far more regulated. Since many industries are not high-emitters, there need not be united capitalist opposition to such policies. This might also provide another phase of "creative destruction," in which low-emissions technologies generate profits and new jobs. Some entrepreneurs are already banking on this and switching into investment in alternative fuels, wetland and forest preservation, and other environmental novelties. At present alternative energy technologies do not create more net jobs in the world, but this might change if they became the norm. A recent report from the Copenhagen Consensus Center suggests that net job gains could be made in the alternative technology sector if several conditions were met: rapid technological innovation, rapid progression of economies of scale, global implementation of similar green policies, and perhaps adoption of protectionist measures such as tariffs or local content requirements. Tax policy could also be directed at job creation. If taxation is levied on the total throughput of nonrenewable resources and not on either business or labor in general, as at present, then that would encourage the hiring of labor. This could be the next wave of creative destruction. It would certainly destroy the fossil fuel industries.

Not only capitalism has to be reined in. We have to also rein in the treadmill of the nation-state's obsession with growth. All nation-states measure national success by GDP growth and yet this increases environmental degradation. That means reining in political elites who believe that they can only retain power by promoting short-term growth within the period of a single electoral cycle. A low-emissions regime would certainly reduce growth in the short run, while hopefully increasing it more in the long run, given that in the long run the do-nothing "business as usual" scenario will prove disastrous for the planet and its inhabitants. But who lives in the long run? Politicians certainly do not and nor do electorates. Moreover politicians and voters still live in the era of nation-state sovereignty where there is great resistance to any curtailment of that sovereignty by foreigners. Yet regulation would have to be international, with intergovernmental agreements severely limiting the autonomy of any nation-state to do its own thing.

Maybe the environmental movement will eventually persuade capitalists, political elites, and voters to begin serious reduction of emissions. Maybe the European Union can lead the way over the sovereignty barrier, since it has already done so in other spheres. But for any of this to happen, we have thirdly to rein in the treadmill of "consumption citizenship" according to which the people demand more and more economic growth in order to consume more, as a citizen right. Ordinary citizens will have to change their lifestyles to avert disaster, but disaster appears abstract and faraway—until it actually happens.

The three great triumphs of the modern period—capitalism, the nation-state, and citizen rights—are responsible for the environmental crisis. These causal chains emanate principally from the economy, though as mediated by political power relations, and the problem is bigger than simply capitalism. All three triumphs would have to be challenged for the sake of a rather abstract future, which is a very tall order, perhaps not achievable. If success were attained, this would reinforce capitalist tendencies toward lower growth. The restrictions would involve much more political regulation, though through international agreements by states acting collectively. It would be a new type of swing away from markets to states, not exactly socialist but a new form of market-regulating suprastate collectivism. The present chances of any of this happening seem slight. America is not only unwilling to begin any of these three struggles but it will not sign up to even minor emissions programs. China does embrace emissions programs and its party rulers have the power to press ahead with them, but all their efforts are overwhelmed by the sheer pace of Chinese industrialization—as is also the case in India and other successfully industrializing countries. I would predict that little emissions mitigation will be undertaken until tangible climate impacts begin to strike hard on the world at some point in the mid-21st century.

Things look torrid on the climate front. Perhaps a technological breakthrough might occur. Neither solar nor wind power are at present offering this, but current experiments with cold fusion, or a radically different solar battery, or concentrated solar power using molten salt, might eventually yield significant results—but not "clean coal," which is just a smokescreen set up by the coal industry. Perhaps the global masses will be stirred up by green movements into persuading politicians into more green policies; perhaps capitalists in low-emissions industries will provide a powerful counterweight to the high-emitters; perhaps entrepreneurs and scientists can jointly pioneer another phase of creative destruction centering on new green technologies. At the moment any of these possibilities is not on the horizon. Of course, if there is an enduring global crisis of capitalism, and world production heads downward, then (after a delay during which already "baked in" emissions will continue upwards) emissions will stop growing and even begin to decline. Conversely, if capitalism, nation-states, and consuming citizens are reined in, then GDP growth will decline through global consensus and everyone will be content with almost zero growth. Every cloud has a silver lining!

But if action is not timely, and climate disaster begins to strike hard, the optimistic scenario would be that at that point the world's states would take coordinated action to impose severe restrictions on capitalism, states and citizens. Alternatively, if this did not occur, various disaster scenarios can be envisioned: of relatively favored states, richer ones in the North of the world, erecting great barriers of "fortress capitalism," "fortress socialism," or "ecofascism" against the rest of the world; of mass refugee starvation; of resource wars (though perhaps not war between nuclear powers). Whether our successors might call these regimes "capitalist," "socialist," "fascist," or whatever, malice would be their ultimately defining character trait. It is of course impossible to predict what human beings will do when confronted by such a threat.

CONCLUSION: THE END MAY OR MAY NOT BE NIGH

I have presented a model of alternative possible scenarios which I believe is the closest we can get to predicting the future. I hope firstly that I have shown that modern society and modern capitalism are not systems. They are influenced by multiple overlapping networks of power, each with their own distinctive causal chains. The most important of these are ideological, economic, military and political. In their possible future interactions some things are clearer than others. First, the United States is losing its hegemonic position in the world—even its enormous military power does not seem able to achieve national interest goals. This seems almost inevitable: the end of hegemony is nigh. Indeed, American power might sink further if its multiple current weaknesses cascading across all four sources of social power are not remedied. Second, the European Union is in a comparably threatened position, though its present economic difficulties are exacerbated mainly by a single political weakness, the unsupported euro. For Europe almost everything depends on solving this problem, which is primarily one of political and ideological rather than economic power. Third, power in the global economy will continue to shift from the West toward the more successful parts of the Rest and on balance this will involve more political regulation of capitalism. All this is fairly clear.

Further scenarios are murkier. If we follow Schumpeter in seeing capitalism as "creative destruction," creation might become the province of the developing Rest, destruction the province of the West. Yet this seems less likely than a return to the multiple power networks of previous eras, this time organized globally. But forces emanating from within the economy will probably not lead to a global crisis of capitalism. More probable is that global economic growth will slow once a more equal distribution of power in the world is reached—a move perhaps toward a stable, prosperous, but low-growth capitalist economy. This would be a rather happy prospect for the world except that it might involve a minority "excluded" class of somewhere between 10% and 20% of the population.

However, all of this might be thrown out of kilter by either of two rogue global crises, nuclear war or escalating climate change, the first of these the result of a causal chain emanating from outside of capitalism, the second of a causal chain bigger than capitalism. Either of these might provide the end, not only of capitalism but also of human civilization. The insects would inherit the earth. But finally, in all these affairs nothing lasts forever and policy decisions matter considerably. Humanity is in principle free to choose between better or worse future scenarios—and so ultimately the future is unpredictable. We sometimes act rationally, though usually only with short-term time horizons, and we sometimes act emotionally, ideologically and irrationally. That is ultimately why we cannot predict the future of either capitalism or the world.

4

WHAT COMMUNISM WAS

Georgi Derluguian

There are obvious reasons for discussing communist states in a book debating the possible demise of capitalist markets. Communism still comes to many minds as the prime alternative to capitalism, along with its dreadful images of endless smokestacks, shortages, personality cults, and purges. There are less obvious reasons, too. The collapse of the Soviet bloc was taken for granted after the fact because communism now seemed to almost everyone patently inefficient and oppressive. Yet in the fifties and sixties prevalent opinions admired/dreaded the extraordinary military and scientific prowess of the U.S.S.R. and even many experts considered its nationality questions solved. During the heady years of Gorbachev's perestroika in the 1980s, many people also, both in the East and West, seemed ready to embrace the humanistic goodness dawning from Moscow. Today the Chinese market miracle is hailed as capitalism's biggest success and hope for the future, disregarding the oddity of many Chinese entrepreneurs still carrying their Party cards. This fact questions the common cliché that communism has ended in collapse.

The Soviet Union, however, did collapse. Toward the end, it became an advanced industrial society ruled by essentially a corporate oligarchy.

Perhaps this allows us to posit on more empirical grounds the question of what the collapse of advanced Western capitalism might look like. Specifically, could a hypothetical anticapitalist revolution follow the classic pattern of 1917, or might it rather resemble the civic mobilizations of 1989? Which brings us to the special reason for considering the Soviet Union in this book. Two of its authors, the same Immanuel Wallerstein and Randall Collins who now predict the end of capitalism, are on record as having predicted, still back in the 1970s and from different theories, the passing of communism in Russia.

Hence my confession: in 1987 I had no authorization from the KGB residentura at our embassy in the People's Republic of Mozambique to meet the US citizen Immanuel Wallerstein. Waiting under the old jacaranda outside Maputo's Hotel Polana felt like stepping into a Graham Greene spy novel: a young Soviet officer secretly meeting with a famous Western academic in an African country torn by Cold War proxy conflict. The intellectual curiosity driving me into this mad risk could be fully appreciated perhaps only by those who knew the excitement of touching a banned book. The Soviet censors regarded Wallerstein's Neo-Marxian theory as, of course, heresy. Sensing my unease, Wallerstein graciously predicted: *Relax, your generation of Soviets will be soon freely traveling around the world, though I am less sure this will make you much happier.* At my incredulous look, he added with a smile: *What makes you expect that there will be a military parade on Moscow's Red Square, let us say safely, on the 7 of November 2017, the hundredth anniversary of an event which by then you might not even know what to call?* The word crossing my mind at that prophetic moment was admittedly a cruder Russian equivalent of *Preposterous!*

Preposterous was also the main reaction of the audience at Columbia University's venerable Russian Institute after the presentation delivered by Randall Collins in spring 1980. The outsider sociologist calmly told the gathering of Sovietologists that, according to his mathematical model, the dark object of their professional interests would disappear in their lifetime. America was still reeling from Vietnam, economic stagflation, and the Iran hostage crisis. Ronald Reagan was campaigning for the presidency on the claim that the United States had fallen dangerously behind the Soviet Union in nuclear armaments and needed a massive arms buildup to contain the communist menace around the globe. And here was Randall Collins, himself son of a career American diplomat, suggesting nuclear disarmament and the continuation of détente. The benign recommendation, however, did not arise from a merely idealistic pacifism. It derived from the geopolitical theory first advanced by Max Weber.[1]

In the Weberian model devised by Randall Collins the U.S.S.R. came out surprisingly negative on all five parameters of geopolitical might. The critical unknown remained in seeing what pattern the Soviet decline would follow. Contrary to the contemporary mood, the same model showed that America in the 1980s was not yet facing geopolitical decline. Therefore the single highest priority for the world and American security was in avoiding a nuclear war with the declining Soviets. The historical precedents of many empires from the past suggested that disintegration from geopolitical overextension typically arrived very suddenly after a period of protracted confrontations gradually reducing the number of belligerents to just two big rivals and their satellites. The structurally weaker empire would then disappear either in an outburst of internal unrest led by separatist governors and weary generals, or in a showdown war fought at unprecedented levels of ferociousness, like Rome versus Carthage.

In all fairness, the Sovietologists had reasons to feel scandalized. Collins drew his empirical evidence from historical atlases of ancient and medieval empires. The geopolitical theory could say little about the latest developments in Poland, Nicaragua, Afghanistan, or Brezhnev's health. Moreover, the prediction of Soviet collapse came with an extremely vague date, some time in the coming decades. Macrosociological predictions tend to be very general. They can only identify the directions of structural drift and roughly estimate their pace. It is doubtful that anyone could do better in the longer run. In fact, the predictions of Sovietology proved worse even in the shorter run.

How do the old predictions of Collins and Wallerstein relate to what we now know about the Soviet trajectory? The present debate on the prospects of capitalism calls for clarity regarding what actually was its communist alternative. But our object is heavily shrouded in ideological polemics.

---

[1] The episode is related in Randall Collins, "Prediction in Macrosociology: The Case of the Soviet Collapse," *American Journal of Sociology* 100.6 (May 1995): 1552–93. The original prediction of Soviet collapse was published by Randall Collins as "Long-Term Social Change and the Territorial Power of States," *Research in Social Movements, Conflict, and Change* 1 (1978): 1–34.

I suggest that a more meaningful way of explaining the rise and demise of communism is by placing it in a larger macrohistorical perspective.

THE RUSSIAN GEOPOLITICAL PLATFORM

The original communist breakthrough achieved on the ruins of Russian empire was an improbable historical contingency. It was, however, no more improbable than the original breakthrough of capitalism in the West or, for that matter, any consequential mutation in the organization of social power. This does not mean that the Bolshevik revolution was a freak event. Historical contingency typically is the human realization of the not yet evident structural opportunities emerging in moments of crisis when previous constraints are breaking down. Creativity and visionary energy—just like blindness to opportunity and failure of leadership—are all the results of human action on the emergent structural possibilities and constraints. The alternatives seem improbable to anyone except, of course, those who will be proclaimed visionaries in hindsight. What such visionaries actually do is discover new possibilities in the course of action and thus turn the possibilities real. Far from all possibilities, however, become reality. The Bolshevik uprising in 1917 closed the small possibility of Russia becoming a liberal democracy. It also closed the much greater possibility of Russia going fascist at the time. Lenin and his small band of comrades obviously mattered a lot in changing the trajectories of Russia and the whole world after 1917. But causality runs in the opposite direction, too. It no less mattered that communist revolutionaries first took over a country like Russia rather than, say, Italy, Mexico, or even China.

In order to appreciate the geopolitical and economic platform called Russia we must go back in history to the nodal points when the Russian empire took its familiar shape. The first such point is found at the dawn of modern era, somewhere between 1500 or 1550. If we polled the contemporary political experts regarding the direction of their world, they would concur above all on the spectacular emergence of new empires across the vast landmass between the Pacific and Atlantic oceans. These imagined experts might hardly mention the Protestant Reformation in the far northwestern extension of Eurasia, perhaps not even the recent discovery of the Americas. Ming China was surely the world's manufacturing and demographic giant. Shortly after 1500 the Mughals imposed their imperial rule in the inherently fractitious India.

At the very same time the Safavis were ascendant in Iran, the Ottoman Turks forcefully reclaimed the legacy of the Eastern Roman Empire, while the Spanish Hapsburgs appeared on their way to establishing a Catholic empire in the West. For almost everyone, the terrible Middle Ages were at last over. The renewed order and prosperity had been secured by the extensive empires and in turn strengthened by a whole range of important innovations: more efficient agrarian and artisanal techniques, bureaucratic taxation, the official conservative religions, and, not in the least, the new big guns.

Russia was a distant outlier in this larger picture. This proved, however, an advantage of sorts. The fledgling empire of the Tsars was protected by sheer geographical distance from its stronger rivals in the west and south, the Germans and Turks. The firearms in the meantime reversed the secular imbalance between nomadic cavalries and sedentary agriculturalists. Securing the Slavic ploughmen against Tatar rovers in the vast fertile lands in the steppe provided sixteenth-century Russia with vastly increased manpower and tribute flows. In its scope and nature, the Russian expansion became comparable only to Spain's. The Cossacks, armed frontiersmen, followed by regular garrisons, traversed the steppe in directions exactly countering the erstwhile nomadic invasions. Soon Russia found itself bordering on China.

It is not so wondrous that in the sixteenth century Russia became an empire along with the many gunpowder empires of its generation; it is more wondrous that in 1900 Russia was still an expanding great power. After all, neither China nor India and Iran, not even Turkey or Spain, could by 1900 preserve their splendid positions. The reason for this massive decline of the rest was obviously related to what had emerged in the intervening centuries from the far West. Spain's impressive bid for the Catholic restoration of Western Roman Empire ran headlong into the collective resistance of lesser kingdoms, principalities, independent cantons, and city leagues of northwestern Europe. Had the Hapsburg monarchy crushed this resistance, the Protestant Reformation would have remained in the historical record as yet another heresy, while the anti-Hapsburg princes and merchants would be considered seditious feudal warlords and seaborne pirates. Of course, the actual course of events awarded a perfectly livable stalemate to the capitalist alliance of Protestant states interlaced by the cosmopolitan merchant networks. It was this military and ideological stalemate rather than the Protestantism in itself that secured the survival of the first capitalist states like the Netherlands and England.

Peter the Great launched his absolutist reformation of Russia only a couple generations after capitalism's breakthrough in the West. The incredible Tsar Peter, who worked in disguise as apprentice carpenter at the Amsterdam shipyards and probably met Isaac Newton in London, was determined to learn from the best. Holland remained Peter's first and most ardent love. To appreciate the power of this hegemonic example one might notice that the flag of Russia is a slightly modified Dutch flag, and the canals of Sankt Pietersburg (the original Dutch spelling) have no other reason than Peter's ferocious belief that a modern capital must have canals like Amsterdam.

Similar reforms by emulation were attempted by many contemporary statesmen: Portugal's Marquês de Pombal, Austria's Emperor Joseph, and, for that matter, Alexander Hamilton in the United States. The rate of success seems to rapidly recede as we move outside the western core. Even Spain eventually lost its imperial possessions and fell into isolation behind the Pyrenees. India, China, and Iran failed outright and slid into foreign dependency. The proudly libertarian and aristocratic Poland-Lithuania, once the biggest European country, disappeared in partitions. The glorious cavalry of Polish feudal *szlachta* was doomed in the new epoch when wars were won by qualitatively more expensive navies, standing armies, and artilleries. The Ottoman Turks gathered force for their Tanzimat reforms a whole century after Petrine Russia, by which time it was too late to shed Turkey's reputation as the "sick man" of Europe. The impressive Albanian Muhammad Ali, the rogue warlord of Egypt, who in 1810–1840 began building his own navy, gun foundries, and modern bureaucracy, comes close to the example of Peter the Great. But the absolutist modernizer of Egypt was soon checked by the British, decidedly unwilling to see a regional power rise in the Middle East astride the projected Suez route to India.

Among the nonwestern states only Japan in the course of its Meiji Restoration after 1868 managed to become a serious force in the military-industrial geopolitics of the age. This odd pairing, Petrine Russia in one century and Meiji Japan in another, possibly suggests a clue. These two very different outliers shared in common an ideological duality of intense national pride with deep-seated insecurity, caused by humiliating confrontations with superior Western forces. Such dualistic perception of their place in the world could be an enabling but not sufficient condition because it was scarcely unique to Japan and Russia. The embattled empires had to gather institutional capacity and finances to act on their anxious sense of backwardness and vulnerability. The relative isolation of Russia and Japan from foreign trade penetration and military pressures afforded both states the breathing space to build up their capabilities and engage in contemporary arms races. The tremendous costs of imperial modernizing burdened mainly the peasants. They had to supply their states with increased taxes, many more laborers on state projects, and army recruits. Coercing the peasants, however, was still not enough. The absolutist reformers had to discipline, re-educate, reward and inspire their own elites by essentially conscripting them wholesale into the state service as military officers and bureaucrats.

This developmentalist pattern was based on the intensive centralization of coercion and territorial expansion bringing in new resources, subject populations, and imperial glories. The standard theory of neoclassical economics extols Anglo-Saxon constitutionalism and private enterprise with secure property rights as the road to modernity. But there obviously was a different way of staying in the running among the contemporary leading states. The alternative coercive strategy compensated for the relative dearth of capitalist resources by turning the state itself into major entrepreneur and fostering modern industries and institutions by decree. Little wonder then that both Japanese and Russian modernizers seeking to emulate the Western advantages typically preferred Germanic examples. The Russian empire since the times of Peter and Catherine the Great had actually imported scores of underemployed German aristocrats and artisans as a developmental boost. This was the peculiar kind of geopolitical platform that the Bolsheviks had seized in 1917.

FORTRESS SOCIALISM

Nobody in 1917 considered the revolution in Russia unexpected. The Russian nobility had long been haunted by the specter of serf peasants revolting to avenge their near-slave condition. A modern proletarian revolution had been awaited ever since the European upheavals of 1848. This fear/hope was fed by strikes of industrial workers met with Cossack cavalry charges. No less significant was the growth of the famous modernist intelligentsia, the middle strata of educated specialists who felt stymied by the old aristocratic bureaucracy and the generalized backwardness of their country. The intelligentsia saw itself as the guiding force of epochal renovation. This sense of lofty mission translated into a spate of subversive strategies, from creating a world-class literature to volunteer charitable activism and throwing bombs at the oppressors.

Nevertheless, the empire kept on muddling through and even registered impressive industrial growth mainly because for almost half a century it had luckily avoided losing wars, a typical trigger of revolutions. The tipping points—as observed in many other revolutions—arrived with the costly and morally embarrassing military defeats in 1905 and again in 1917. The soldiers rebelled against their commanders while the police disintegrated. The collapse of state coercion released all the long-repressed specters of rebellion: furious peasant revolts in the countryside; the now armed worker militancy in big cities; the intelligentsia enthusiastically organizing a panoply of political parties and nationalist movements that soon became independent governments in the ethnically non-Russian provinces.

It is not too surprising that the Bolsheviks seized power amidst this breakdown of state order. It is truly surprising that they were still in power a few years later. How did they do it? The Bolsheviks before 1917 were a small insurrectionist current of intelligentsia. The conditions of illegality and persecution engendered among them strict internal discipline, conspiratorial secrecy, and vigilance against the ever-present police spies. Unlike their Chinese counterparts, the Bolsheviks were not guerrillas and had virtually no presence outside the big towns. This supported their prejudiced view of peasants as an uneducated mass to be marched into a better future. And, of course, the almost religious devotion of the Bolsheviks to the cause followed the eschatological vision of Karl Marx. But Marxism also carried a powerful scientific side. This made the Bolsheviks a peculiarly rationalist kind of ideological visionaries enamored with modern science and industry. From the outset, these anticapitalist and anti-imperialist Marxist revolutionaries were prepared to take up the weapons of their enemies: German military organization, state industrial planning, and the production lines of Henry Ford.

The Bolshevik party in power first grew its own secret police: the infamous Cheka, which absorbed scores of revolutionary terrorists. This ensured the internal political monopoly of the fledgling state. Next the party created its own Red Army. Forging an army amidst civil war and foreign military interventions more than safeguarded the Bolshevik state; it essentially became the Bolshevik state. The spirited and disciplined party-in-arms also proved eminently adapted for organizing all sorts of rear support and moral boosters: making the collapsing industries run, requisitioning food from peasants, but also, in the Enlightenment élan of intelligentsia, opening museums, theaters, literacy courses, and universities.

One key aspect of Bolshevik state-building, however, was unprecedented for a polyglot empire: national republics constituting the Soviet Union. The multisided civil war was won by forging political and military alliances across the dividing lines of nationality, race, and religion. In a critical episode during 1919, the counterrevolutionary White Army of General Anton Denikin was hit from the rear by Muslim Chechen fighters who had allied with the Bolsheviks in the belief that Marxism was also a form of jihad. The Caucasus Muslim rebels might have seemed politically naïve. Yet the Bolsheviks earnestly meant development for the non-Russian periphery, albeit on their own terms. The Leninist nationality policy institutionalized the national republics where native cadres could enjoy promotion preferences and considerable resources to build the institutions of modern ethnic cultures: the same schools and universities, museums, film studios, opera and ballet but specifically destined for the non-Russian nationalities.

The Bolshevik victory in the Russian Civil War cannot be reduced to creating state order out of chaos, although in itself this was an inordinate achievement. The lesson was rather in forging the extensive structures that harnessed and directed the emotional energies of the millions touched by revolution. These masses of young men and women suddenly saw their life chances dramatically expanded by the technical education and promotions available within the new Soviet institutions. The opportunities for social mobility grew exponentially once the furiously massive construction of new industries and towns was launched in the early 1930s. For all their brutal daily austerity, political terror, and inhuman workloads, the industrialization and Second World War also produced a mass constituency of patriotic Soviet citizens with new identities and lifestyles generated by a vast modernistic state. The demolition of old communities, churches, and extended patriarchal families released millions of younger men and women into the wider modern society. On a wholly different scale, the effect resembled the eighteenth-century westernization of Peter the Great (who was lionized in Soviet novels and films). The Petrine absolutism succeeded in its own epoch by multiplying the ranks of nobility and endowing the new elite with ample service opportunities, ideological confidence, and Westernized lifestyles. In the Soviet era the children of peasants, both Russian and ethnically non-Russian, could learn to operate modern machinery, move into state-built apartments with running water and electricity, acquire new Soviet-made watches and radios, and lunch in workplace canteens on industrially produced hot dogs, canned peas, mayonnaise salad, and ice cream (these originally American imports soon became regarded as dearly native). State-led industrialization created a perennially overheated economy of pervasive shortages including the shortage of skilled labor. The Soviet Union in effect became a giant factory and therefore it had to become a gigantic company town, too, where the state as sole employer provided social welfare from cradle to grave.

Directing the transformations were party cadres from the special appointment rosters called *nomenklatura*. Eventually the name nomenklatura would become a pejorative for stolid bureaucrats. Its first generations, however, were the battle-hardened youthful commissars and emergency managers full of revolutionary charisma and "can-do" spirit. They believed that incredible historical fortune—and Lenin's genius—had advanced them into the vanguard of humanity's progress. Losing their political power even temporarily, like in an electoral democracy, was tantamount to betraying the march of history. The Bolshevik revolutionary atrocities and their Enlightenment enthusiasm appeared to many commentators and historians impossible to reconcile on moral grounds. Both aspects of communism are incontrovertible facts; it is the perceived contradiction that is an ideological illusion. The Russian revolution imposed a comparatively thin layer of radical intelligentsia over a huge predominantly peasant country. These activists of epochal change ardently believed in electricity and universal progress, but they had also learned in the recent civil war to trust the victorious Party and rely on the cherished Mauser handguns. In short, Russian revolutionaries won their battles by becoming an unprecedented charismatic bureaucracy. These militant developmentalists fused the ideological, political, military, and economic institutions of the twentieth century into a single dictatorial structure. Its summit amounted to a high pedestal.

Stalin's personality was perhaps as twisted as his amazing life trajectory of a latter-day catacomb Christian becoming Great Inquisitor and later a Renaissance Pope, too. Yet personality does not explain the leader cults and purges in many situations where Stalin could not be a direct culprit, such as Tito's Yugoslavia, Maoist China, and Cuba. Or consider, for that matter, Gorbachev's *glasnost* campaign that between 1985 and 1989 cost the jobs if not the lives of nearly two-thirds of the Brezhnev-era nomenklatura. From the perspective of bureaucratic victims, the Moscow-mandated democratization amounted to another calamitous purge. This realization, as we shall see, goes a long way toward explaining the desperately defensive and destructive reactions of Soviet nomeklatura that would ruin the state after 1989. All great communist leaders/villains periodically unleashed campaigns of political denunciation because less blunt mechanisms of control were unavailable to them. The suppression of unofficial organizing and information leaves the supreme leader essentially blind to whatever is happening under his feet and rightly suspicious that his commands are not fully implemented.

This ugly feature of Leninist regimes had no direct relation to Russian, Chinese, or any national culture. It would have certainly appalled Karl Marx, maybe even Lenin himself. The problem, however, was rooted right in the geopolitical origins of communist states (and, we may add, their non-Marxist nationalist emulators across the Third World). These revolutionary states were born in deadly confrontations. Great leaders emerged at their summit because the extraordinary national mobilizations called for supreme military, political, and economic commanders. Their genius then appeared validated by their great improbable victories. Napoleon Bonaparte truly served as the historical prototype for all revolutionary emperors of the twentieth century.

The revolutions capturing single states, even as big as Russia, would immediately run into interstate rivalries. Hence the typical modern sequence of successful revolutions followed by external war. Revolutionary transformations provoked military confrontations with other states that were either seeking to preserve the conservative status quo or, as in the case of the Third Reich, intending to remake the world through a war of conquest and extermination. The emergence of communist states in the twentieth century was a major achievement of leftist forces. But, given the terrible wars amidst which the communist and national liberation insurgents could take power, from the inception their regimes grew oppressive and institutionally flawed. The twentieth-century revolutionaries had no other course of action if they intended to defend and consolidate their antisystemic conquests. If one needs a big rationalist argument for curbing militarism, then there it is.

Was the Soviet Union genuinely socialist or was it rather totalitarian? Such exceedingly ideological abstractions are not useful in explaining reality. It was what it was: a huge centralized state with an unusual ideology and a formidable military-geopolitical position achieved as the result of extraordinary industrialization. The geopolitical inheritance of Russian empire, uniquely strong in the world's semiperipheral zone, made possible the survival of such a state in the first place. The same structural inheritance also suggested the state-driven coercive strategy of industrialization predicated on dispossessing the peasantry and putting every effort into building an up-to-date military force.

The U.S.S.R. was quintessentially modern and self-consciously modernist. It successfully adopted the advanced power techniques of its age: mechanized military, assembly line industry, planned big towns, mass education and social welfare, and standardized mass consumption including sports and entertainment. After the futuristic decade of the 1920s, the Bolsheviks would also recycle as new mass culture the classical music, ballet, and literature inherited from the imperial intelligentsia. The Stalinist state had indeed ended up looking imperial in many respects. Yet the ability of the U.S.S.R. to integrate its numerous nationalities for almost three generations was arguably progressive and modernistic. The Soviets pioneered affirmative action and then proved by development and broad inclusion that they really meant it.

At the time many observers, friend and foe alike, tended to agree that these achievements based on economic planning and the abolition of private property in sum amounted to socialism. The key Soviet features were emulated or reinvented by a broad variety of developmentalist and nationalist regimes because such a concentration of state powers appeared extraordinarily successful for the duration of twentieth century. Here we find a number of former empires whose peoples were hoping to redeem their historical humiliations and claim a better, stronger position in the world: the communist partisan states of China, Yugoslavia, and Vietnam, but also nationalist Turkey and, later, Iran, with its peculiar antisystemic ideology of Islamic nationalism. Even the small, defiant Cuba and, on the opposite side of the Cold War divide, the most peculiar State of Israel added to the variety of insurgent nationalisms adopting the features of "fortress socialism."

All such states faced hostile geopolitics. After the initial periods of revolutionary romanticism, the world-system's structural realities kicked in with hard policy choices: spontaneity versus discipline, idealists versus enforcers, inspiring the masses or coercing the peasants, ideological purity fraught with perilous isolation or uneasy international alliances. If communists wanted to be serious players on the world stage, their effective response had to be opportunistic realpolitik. Despite ideological proclamations, communist states could never totally quit the capitalist world-system. Conflict is in fact one of the strongest kinds of ties in social networks, be it at the level of small groups or among the states. The core capitalist states continued to be the main preoccupation and reference point for Moscow. Germany before 1945 and America ever after posed the main military menace dictating the priorities of Soviet industry and science. But the West also remained the vital source for buying advanced machinery and prestigious goods with the earnings obtained mainly from the export of raw materials. The once endless debates about communist alternative have been ultimately ended by the fact that all communist states, one way or another, eventually reverted to capitalism.

THE COSTS OF DEVELOPMENTAL SUCCESS

This brings us back to the old predictions of Randall Collins and Immanuel Wallerstein. Their ability to see the coming end of communism derived from very different theories and focused on different processes: geopolitical over-extension for Collins, and the structural imperatives of the capitalist world-economy for Wallerstein. The predictions, however, reinforced each other in interesting ways. Collins saw two dire outcomes to the Soviet dilemma of overextension: imperial disintegration or an all-out war of last resort. Wallerstein identified the third possibility in a pan-European economic and military bloc emerging around the axis of Paris—Berlin—Moscow. This scenario evidently conformed to the long-standing ambitions of Charles de Gaulle and the hopeful spirit of the 1970s German *Neue Ostpolitik*. Analytically, Wallerstein's unrealized prediction directs our attention to an important counterfactual. It posits Mikhail Gorbachev's perestroika as a viable possibility. Incidentally, this counterfactual still implies that a rebuilt Russia and the EU can find structural reasons to form a military and economic bloc in the near future. The past predictions of Collins and Wallerstein, however, were abstract sketches that left a lot to be filled in regarding the shifting social forces, specific mechanisms, and event sequences leading to the observed as well as aborted historical outcomes.

Randall Collins derived his prediction from extending into future the dynamics of great geopolitical turmoil in Europe between 1914 and 1945 that had removed the majority of Russia's erstwhile adversaries. The sweeping simplification of world geopolitics after 1945 from complex multipolarity to a Cold War binary opposition of just two ideological blocs turned the Soviet Union into a superpower. But such a position also brought costs and liabilities at an unprecedented scale. In the continuing confrontation with America, reasoned Randall Collins back in 1980, the U.S.S.R. had already reached the tipping point at which the costs of controlling allies and confronting external rivals must become insuperable.

In an important corollary, the same model predicted China's potential for economic prosperity. At the time almost nobody took seriously this huge reservoir of Asiatic poverty presided by idiosyncratic Chairman Mao. The side effects of superpower rivalry, however, left China in a lucky kind of geopolitical limbo. The eccentric communist state in East Asia by the late 1970s found itself in a constraining but also stable interstate environment where its geopolitical costs seemed very minor in comparison to Soviet costs. Chinese leaders, like the leaders of Japan after 1945, were left to pursue the state goals of power and prestige through the path most obvious in their region at the time—the export-oriented industrialization dependent on the American consumer markets.

Immanuel Wallerstein had been long (and very controversially) comparing communist states to factories seized by a labor union during a strike.[2] If the workers try to operate the factory themselves, they inevitably have to follow the rules of capitalist markets. The workers might get a better distribution of material rewards, but not equality or democracy. The more "realist" among labor organizers would reimpose production discipline, compellingly citing external market pressures. The "Iron Law of Oligarchy" in complex organizations predicted that the narrow circle of those making managerial decisions would cut themselves off from the larger group and evolve into a new ruling elite. It might take time before ideological vapor entirely escaped from the cauldrons. Nevertheless the moment would

---

[2] There are many essays and books where Immanuel Wallerstein discusses the U.S.S.R. in world-systemic perspective. See his 1973 programmatic essay "The Rise and Future Demise of the World Capitalist System" reprinted in the *Essential Wallerstein* (New York: New Press, 2000), 71–105. Also see Wallerstein's paper co-authored in the spring of 1991 (i.e., before the Soviet collapse) with Giovanni Arrighi and Terence Hopkins, "1989, The Continuation of 1968," *REVIEW* 15.2, (1992) 221–42.

come when the erstwhile organizers turned managers would no longer feel compelled to disguise the reality. The factory would then revert to being a normal capitalist enterprise, and the managers would cash in on their positions. If you wish, it is a sociological version of George Orwell's *Animal Farm*, but Wallerstein's analysis specified in a clear and logical fashion the structural conditions and causal sequences. He also added an important political caveat: socialism in one country or one factory may not last unless the whole capitalist world-system is replaced by a different historical system where capital accumulation is no longer the paramount priority.

Wallerstein based his metaphor of the union-controlled factory rejoining capitalism on the actually observed facts. Soviet leaders tried to trade their ideological and military positions for economic integration with the West as early as 1953. Days after Stalin's death, the dreadful head of secret police Lavrenty Beria ordered the first massive release of inmates from the Gulag and signaled to the West Moscow's willingness to withdraw from East Germany. This short-lived episode points to a curious possibility. Beria was known to be an utterly cynical opportunist but also a ruthlessly pragmatic economic manager. Had he succeeded, communism would have likely ended much sooner. Beria would probably have ruled as a personalistic dictator selectively allowing his cronies to share in the capitalist profits at the time when Soviet industries and newly educated labor were just entering their prime. This could have outdone the market recovery of China after the death of Mao. Imagine Western consumers driving today the stylish Soviet-made *Volgas* and wearing *Vostok* watches. But in 1953 the unification of Germany was a broadly unwanted proposition in the Western alliance, and Europe had plenty of its own skilled eager workers emerging from the decades of war and depression.

In historical reality Beria was arrested and executed by his Politburo rivals. It was the revenge of party nomenklatura and military commanders for the fear and humiliations at the hands of secret police. In 1956 the new Soviet leader Nikita Khrushchev denounced the crimes of Stalin—and merrily survived this indiscretion. He would be toppled in 1964 only after attempting to undo the bastions of bureaucratic intransigence in the gigantic vertically integrated industrial ministries, the Soviet equivalent of economic corporations. The nomenklatura cadres certainly desired a limited de-Stalinization. But they wanted to stop the changes once officialdom had achieved their bureaucratic paradise of life tenure, generous perks, and a more relaxed work pace. The sprawling command apparatus of economic ministries, dating back to the industrial spurt of 1930s, thus perpetuated itself essentially unchanged. Its parts would survive even the Soviet collapse of 1991, ensuring that postcommunist capitalism acquired a distinctly oligarchic character of tremendous wealth concentration and corrupt insider politics.

The costs of bureaucratic self-incorporation were transpiring already after the death of Stalin. Command economy must have its Supreme Commander who makes decisions regarding the allocation of resources. In his absence central government is reduced to bureaucratic inertia amidst the corporate lobbying of influential ministries and territorial governments. The old economic debate about the virtues of plan versus market is based on the timeless and therefore false assumption that these are mutually exclusive ideological choices. Planned or rather command economies could be more effective in the short run when time demanded delivering the miracles of large-scale standardized production, such as required during wars, postdisaster recoveries, or industrialization leaps. The command model, however, is unsuited for the longer and more normal periods that require more diversified and flexible adaptations. But how could anyone dare suggest scrapping the giant obsolescent enterprise that was the pride of the first Five-Year Plans and whose top managers, incidentally, were voting members in the Central Committee? This is precisely what toppled Nikita Khrushchev in 1964. The Soviet executives and ideologues grew as intolerant of market ideas as their capitalist counterparts in the age of neoliberalism would grow intolerant of public property and regulation. The intransigence of industrial and political bosses, however, had deeper reasons than orthodoxy alone. In the main, it was the fear that their better-educated and energetic younger subalterns were bound to unseat the seniors if open discussion and competition were allowed.

The main tension of Soviet communism in its late period pitted the now stolidly bureaucratized nomenklatura against the rising middle strata of educated specialists and creative intellectuals. The new youthful groups of the romantic "sixtiers" emerged from the lower and middle ranks of the state institutions of economic planning, higher education, and culture. In a quite literal sense, these were the children of Soviet modernization. The original ideology of young specialists was a version of the New Left movements emerging all over the world between 1956 and 1968. Only much later, during the crisis of Gorbachev's perestroika, would the antibureaucratic frustrations of junior echelons find a radically different expression in the individualistic philosophy of neoliberalism or in the affirmation of their ethnic nationalisms. The official antisystemic ideology of the Soviet bloc thus suggested to youthful rebels the adoption of Western systemic ideologies, and then, by logic of polarization, in their most extreme versions.

In no social arena did this process emerge as vigorously as in culture. The official orthodoxy prescribes "socialist realism"? Give them absurdist comedies and spiritualist mysticism! The nomenklatura extol friendship among the peoples? Then play on the local ethnic sentiments. The Ministry of Culture enforces the classicist canon in music and arts? Bring forth abstractionism, jazz and rock. The irony is, of course, that the ageing dictatorial regime that stopped acting as a dictatorship became a perfect target for youthful pranks and provocations. The now sclerotic generation of obedient Soviet bureaucrats formed in the end of Stalinist purges could never incorporate this iconoclastic enthusiasm, as the Bolsheviks could in earlier generations.

Just as it could not reign in the intelligentsia, the Soviet regime in its later stage failed to make the workers work. The immediate reason was political. Having reigned in the secret police for the sake of their own safety, the nomenklatura were least of all willing to unleash again any kind of mass repression. In the meantime the expansive industrial economy precluded the disciplining whip of unemployment. The Soviet managers needed labor to accomplish the plan assignments, and workers could in effect bargain for better conditions or seek them elsewhere in the specially supplied Moscow or in the generously paying industries of Siberia.

Yet by far the biggest structural reason giving more power to Soviet workers was demographic transition. The villages of central Russia now stood drained of manpower. By default, this situation significantly increased the social power of women. In the meantime towns, industrial employment, and education irreversibly changed their lifestyles, and birthrates plummeted in merely a generation. The shortage of labor was historically unprecedented in Russia. The tsars and even Stalin could always rely on a seemingly endless supply of peasant labor and army recruits. In the 1960s the demographic pool had suddenly dried up. Recasting peasants into workers was in fact the triumph of Soviet civilization. It also meant the undoing of the centuries-old Russian tradition of supporting the elites and competing militarily with the West at the expense of the peasantry. Relative demographic scarcity left no grounds for traditional despotism.

The formation of Soviet industrial society and its new demographic dynamic fostered two structural preconditions for changing the now hopelessly obsolete structures of Soviet militarized industrialism. The emergent democratization, however, still needed the third and explicitly political condition if it were to overpower the despotic nomenklatura. It was an alliance between the liberal intelligentsia and professionals with the newly empowered labor. In fact, this kind of broad democratic alliance had already proven its force in the explosive popular mobilizations of Czechoslovakia in 1968 and Poland in 1980. The post-Stalinist regimes seemed and indeed felt extremely vulnerable to the leftist popular uprisings because they have lost or willingly retired their ideological and coercive resources to confront the challenge of social movements with massive violence. Yet class conflict in a mature industrial society, contrary to the classical Marxist imagery, was not two-sided. It was rather played out in the triangle of Soviet corporate executives, liberal intelligentsia, and workers. Therefore the nomenklatura's best option was to buy off the workers at the expense of the intelligentsia.

The political taming of Soviet workers in the Brezhnev period was secured with two costly tactics: increased popular consumption and the tacit toleration of inefficiencies. The nomenklatura essentially invited the workers to share in their own complacency and perks while at the same time denigrating the engineers and intellectuals and occasionally bashing dissident intelligentsia for their "rootless cosmopolitanism." The windfall of petrodollars in the 1970s comfortably subsidized this conservative welfare compact for more than two decades. Its true costs defy material estimation. The notorious rises in alcoholism, male mortality, and petty theft from the workplace, along with the shoddy quality of Soviet goods, all must be regarded as the pathological consequences of lost dynamism and pervasive cynicism. It was this avoidance of consequences and a social immobilism stifling the young that came to be despised in the Brezhnev "decades of stagnation."

How Inevitable the Collapse?

The long-awaited energetic younger leader Mikhail Gorbachev belonged to the generation of Sputnik and de-Stalinization. These achievements of the early sixties had experientially validated the belief of his peers in the Soviet system. Gorbachev might be even considered a part of the New Left resurgence from the sixties. Yet he also came heavily invested in the official positions of authoritarian power and, objectively speaking, his goals were quite conservative. By taking the Soviet bloc into state capitalism, he was hoping essentially to strengthen the existing political structures and recast at least the younger nomenklatura into technocratic managers of large industrial holdings with foreign participation. These were the contradictions that rendered Gorbachev's ebullient rhetoric so confusing to his prospective supporters and fatally confused the last General Secretary himself. Few observers believed at the time that Gorbachev really meant what he was saying, but everybody assumed that this seasoned apparatchik knew what he was doing. The truth, as it happens, was exactly the opposite. Gorbachev's policies looked so haphazard and amateurish because the decades-long suppression of policy debate had produced in the U.S.S.R. a highly charged ideological polarization. Between the ritualistic wooden discourse of the Party and the abstract humanism of the dissidents lay a vacuum of ideas and practical solutions. Amateurish improvisation was what remained to the political leader intent on any serious reform.

But imagine for a moment that Gorbachev had succeeded. Extending the key vectors of his policies gives us a fairly plausible end destination. The U.S.S.R. abandons its widespread commitments across the Third World and withdraws from Eastern Europe. From the standpoint of Moscow, this would not be such a loss given that Poland and Czechoslovakia would soon find themselves between the unified Germany and its strategic economic partner Russia. Disarmament deals with America dramatically reduce geopolitical burdens, at last allowing Moscow to restructure its military-industrial complex. The Soviet industries, still formidable and staffed by skilled and comparatively low-paid labor, attract West European investments through government-brokered contracts. (The Soviet managers always felt intuitively close to their German, French, and Italian counterparts embodying broadly similar state-corporatist dispositions.) Pent-up consumer demand in the former communist countries, coupled with job creation, soon generates a big economic upswing. The communist parties perhaps become split into ruling majorities of moderate social democrats and isolated minorities of ideological stalwarts. The entire European continent from the Urals to the Atlantic is unified in a single geopolitical and economic bloc, with Germany as its economic engine and Russia as the supplier of labor, raw materials, and military force. In this version of events, American hegemony fades away much sooner from world geopolitics. A social democratic and paternalistic

Europe together with a recast U.S.S.R. would have enough reasons and power to oppose the neoliberal Washington consensus. The geopolitically and ideologically marginalized America, however, would not be doing too badly economically. Given the strengths of the European example, Washington might find the spirit to adopt the political measures necessary to generate internal demand and establish its own trading bloc with Latin America and China. The world in this case remains certainly capitalist but it would be a different variety and configuration of capitalist globalization.

If the world had gone down this pathway, Gorbachev would now appear the political "sphinx" astutely placating different constituencies with his opaque messages. The visionary pragmatist then would have been praised for taking his country "across the river feeling with his foot one stone at a time" to the shores of capitalist prosperity. The river-crossing metaphor is, of course, Chinese, and it refers to Deng Xiaoping. It is perhaps worth remembering that until the end of 1989, or even later, Gorbachev was universally praised as democracy promoter and the bold unifier of Europe, while Deng was vilified as the butcher of Tiananmen Square. The difference between the Chinese and Soviet exits from communism, however, was not only in the leading personalities and their political styles. There existed plenty of structural differences, the majority of them historically inherited, contingent, and generally unrelated to communism.

In two very different ways, the year 1989 marked the extinction of communism. The Soviet Union fell even faster than China rose. The People's Republic of China also had experienced its close call in the spring of 1989 when an emergent factional split at the top of communist hierarchy had provoked the student movement symbolically associated with Beijing's Tiananmen Square. The student movement displayed the same strengths and weaknesses as the contemporary antiauthoritarian movements in the Soviet Union or, for that matter, the western New Left in 1968 and the Arab Spring of 2011. The spontaneous protest delivered a huge charge of youthful emotional energy directed primarily at the hypocritical and self-serving elders. But the movement lacked an extensive autonomous organization, short-term political goals, and robust connection to provincial towns, let alone the countryside. In 1989 the Chinese party cadres closed their ranks against the movement because the previous episode of upper-echelon factionalism provoking student militancy, the ultra-Maoist Cultural Revolution of the late 1960s, was very much in their memory. Perhaps more importantly, senior Chinese cadres remained the veterans of armed struggle—unlike Gorbachev and his comrades who were career apparatchiks two generations removed from revolution and civil war. For people like Deng Xiaoping, the notion of power growing from a gun barrel was not merely a metaphor.

The suppression of the Tiananmen protests, however, came at a steep ideological cost. The activist students laid claim on the same ideals that legitimated the Communist party itself. The leftist attack on a leftist regime produced a turn to the right even if nobody from the top ever dared to officially acknowledge it. In effect, 1989 marked the end of Chinese communism, too. The ruling CCP quietly put aside its dangerously double-sided ideology and shifted instead to what might be called performance-based legitimacy. This was in fact a well-known move in the policy repertoire of communist regimes. As early as in 1921 the Russian Bolsheviks, ever mindful of past revolutionary precedents, had been coyly admitting that their market-driven New Economic Policy (NEP) meant the necessary phase of "auto-Thermidorean restoration" in revolutionary sequence. In other words, we better liberalize ourselves, as temporary retreat and ahead of the class enemies. Also recall the once famous examples of Tito's Yugoslavia and Janos Kadar's Hungary in the 1960s that combined various market experiments with targeted political repression. Even the uneventful reign of Leonid Brezhnev in the Soviet Union, in retrospect nostalgically remembered as the "good decades," in fact meant a conservative reaction to the boisterous and unsettling period of Khrushchev's Thaw. In the 1970s Soviet leaders, however, ended any talk of market socialism because the export earnings from oil and natural gas afforded them the transient luxury of a risk-free bureaucratic inertia.

Post-Maoist China, of course, had little oil to export. Instead, the CCP could draw for its latter-day NEP from the human ocean of industrious peasants and provincial artisans as well as the market knowledge of the Chinese diaspora. The immediately political rationale for admitting market forces into the Chinese countryside and export zones was clear and simple: to let the peasants feed themselves and the cities in order to defuse tensions. By making this first defensive step, the Chinese communists stumbled on the long road that led them to bypass the political crisis of 1989. Still nominally communist, China essentially reproduced at a greater scale the earlier pattern of anticommunist developmental states in East Asia, such as South Korea and Taiwan, which had grown under the Cold War patronage of American hegemony.

The inadvertently lucky escape of Chinese communism helps us to pinpoint the causes of the Soviet inadvertent disaster. It was, overall, a colossal failure of collective action on the part of nomenklatura. The avalanche of political events in 1989 caused panic and numerous defections from the ranks of Soviet officialdom. It was they who actually undid their own state—not the romantic nationalists in the non-Russian republics, nor the democratic intelligentsia in Moscow and Leningrad. The antinomenklatura insurgents, for all their emotional appeal, had not yet gathered force to overthrow communism on their own. In 1989 and still in 1991 they were lacking serious organizational bases to rapidly mobilize and intercept the falling political power.

Surprisingly enough, neither could the Soviet nomenklatura rely on any legitimate overarching networks to coordinate their self-defenses at a critical moment. During the years of perestroika in 1985–1989, Mikhail Gorbachev had been astutely using his supreme powers as General Secretary to safeguard himself from the bureaucratic backlash of the kind that had buried Nikita Khrushchev. Gorbachev's maneuvering, conducted both in public (i.e., glasnost) and in the insider apparat intrigues, in which he was reputedly so adept, confused and immobilized all three institutional pillars of Soviet regime: the Communist Party, central ministries, and secret police. But in 1989 Gorbachev's inevitable sacrifice of the satellite communist regimes in Eastern Europe suddenly revealed to the embattled nomenklatura their true stakes in this big and uncertain game. Following 1989, the Soviet oligarchic elite fragmented exactly along the lines of bureaucratic turf in the industrial sectors and national republics. For the first time since the legendary 1920s, various political factions appeared within and around the Communist party. But these factions, progressive and reactionary alike, proved short-lived because in the rapidly unwinding chaos they had very little time to pull themselves together. By default, the nomenklatura were left with what they actually knew very well: the elementary personalistic networks of corruption and collusion. At the time, this process seemed utterly chaotic—yet it was not entirely random.

The nomenklatura represented the top echelon of bureaucratic administration. This is why they were all hierarchically subordinated and in principle removable. As in any big managerial bureaucracy, the secrets of survival had always been extending the insider networks of patronage connections, accruing lobbying weight, and protecting the turfs. After 1989 these survival strategies were opportunistically pushed to a totally new scale. The

nomenklatura existed in three intersecting hierarchies: territorial governments (including ethnic autonomies), economic branch ministries, and the
central controlling apparatus of the secret police and the party's ideological "inquisition." Among the three, the controlling hierarchy had been pre-
eminent, yet it also proved the most difficult to privatize. After all, a secret
police without a state becomes a mafia, and ideological "inquisition" without a ruling party is reduced to a sulking sect. The territorial and economic
units of the former U.S.S.R., by comparison, proved fabulously endowed for
the self-aggrandizing separatism. Who could now remove a national president for life or a private capitalist oligarch with his assets stashed away in an
exotic tax haven?

The Soviet industrial assets by various brutally simple schemes were
snatched into private control (admittedly a mild way of saying stolen)
even before privatization was sanctioned by any legislation. Meanwhile national republics and city halls also became corporate property of the kind
that Americans call "political machines." Ironically, the liberal intelligentsia
themselves suggested these new strategies along with their ideological jus-
tifications. The nascent "civil societies" (in practice, the networks of intelligentsia usually limited to capital cities) were now aspiring to turn their
countries into liberal democracies bound to join the capitalist West on their
own, bypassing Moscow and its mumbling, outpaced Gorbachev. This rapid
ideological drift, from the erstwhile New Left and reform communism to
the creed of Margaret Thatcher, reflected the radicalization of demands
typical of any revolution. After 1989 the insurgent intelligentsia were demanding three things: free elections, national sovereignty, and markets. All
three demands were construed as battering rams against ruling bureaucracy
and the means of miraculously emancipating the popular initiatives. But
the governors of the Soviet republics, who had witnessed 1989 in Eastern
Europe, also realized that preemptive declarations of sovereignty could help
to ensure them against removal by Gorbachev in his ongoing "rejuvenation
of cadres" (read: purge). Early elections in the meantime often allowed the
nomenklatura incumbents to outrun the loud but ideologically utopian intelligentsia. Market privatization then splendidly served the old/new presi-
dents who doled out fabulous deals to their relatives and clients.

The mass defection of the former nomenklatura and their vertiginous
self-recasting into capitalists and nationalists wrought havoc in state and economic structures. Ethnic wars flared up along the southern periphery of

the collapsing Soviet Union. Even in the heartlands, amidst the breakdown of public order, the running nomenklatura had to fear for their lives or cut dirty deals with the Mafioso violent entrepreneurs. Such outcomes travestied Gorbachev's intents. His aim was to negotiate from the position of superpower strength an advantageous collective inclusion in the capitalist networks of Western Europe. But the former Soviet republics rapidly lost the advantages of a strong military and international prestige, advanced science, and public order. The dramatic weakening of successor states made impossible any kind of directed industrial development.

The Soviet Union fostered a mono-organizational industrial society where all spheres of public activity were centrally directed. The loss of state integrity undermined all modern institutions and therefore disabled collective action at practically any level above family and crony networks. This condition became self-perpetuating. Individually the most rational and rewarding course of action now suggested looting the state assets and ferreting the loot abroad after a few lucky runs. The rulers themselves were eminently complicit in the weakening of their states because corruptible officials and impotent judiciary became the necessary conditions for looting and personalistic patronage. Such traditional concerns of state power as military strength and containing internal protests became largely irrelevant in the world geopolitics policed by the hegemonic America and institutions of global finance. All the former Soviet states compliantly proclaimed themselves market democracies, albeit with various "national specificities" clumsily excusing the primitive monopolism of their rulers.

Privatizations dealt a crushing blow to the once boisterous intelligentsias whose prestigious secure jobs and professional networks were embedded in state institutions. Liberal intellectuals, and even especially the social critics, found themselves shamefully impoverished, politically outmaneuvered, and ideologically speechless because their liberal and nationalist programs had been cynically hijacked. Moreover the shift of elite power strategies from state-run industrial production and military aggrandizement to private security, commodity exports, and financial speculation had the further perverse effect of insulating the postcommunist oligarchies from the rest of citizenry. The specialists and workers lost their collective leverage as productive labor and patriotic army recruits, or even as voters and taxpayers. What sense did it now make to organize strikes at bankrupt factories, march in the streets under the discredited slogans of national independence and market reform, or campaign for the politicians who would all become traitors? The perestroika-period atmosphere of public empowerment and optimistic anticipation abruptly changed to apathetic cynicism, preoccupations with economic hardship and criminality, and the desperate desire to emigrate. Instead of the promised land of Western Europe, the post-Soviets ended up closer to the harsher realities of the Middle East.

Predictions and Historical Pathways

Randall Collins and Immanuel Wallerstein overall correctly discerned the structural trends pointing to the imminent end of communism. Collins highlighted the paradox of geopolitical limitations to Soviet power when it appeared at the pinnacle of expansion. He was also right in predicting the pattern of collapse suddenly emerging from the massive defection of subordinate elites in the national republics and satellite states in reaction to the political incapacitation of imperial center. But the model of Randall Collins anticipated neither speed nor the direction of Moscow's action on its superpower dilemmas.

Wallerstein went further in his analysis of available options and argued that the best possible destination of Soviet reforms would be a negotiated return to capitalism under a pan-continental European alliance. In the Cold War atmosphere virtually nobody including the Soviet reformers themselves seriously calculated on this possibility. Wallerstein, however, underestimated the burdens of institutional complexity embedded in the ethnic federalism and industrial ministries of the U.S.S.R. The fragmented successors did all revert to capitalism, albeit of a weaker peripheral variety. Instead of rationally bargaining on superpower advantages for a more honorable collective inclusion in the world capitalist hierarchy, the nomenklatura squandered and cannibalized Soviet assets in a panicked rush to protect the individual oligarchic positions against both Gorbachev's purging and the prospect of popular rebellions. Wallerstein's theory was fundamentally correct because of its macroperspective on world capitalism; and for the same macroscopic reason it failed to envision the embarrassing political failure of Soviet elites to act together in the pursuit of their best historical opportunity. This should serve us a stark warning: oligarchic elites, especially when institutionally disunited and blinded by ideological prejudice, can grievously botch their transitions.

Contrary to the dominant Left/Right beliefs of the time, measuring the Soviets against ideological yardsticks, the analyses of Collins and Wallerstein proved overall to be correct because they were systemic and relational. In other words, they considered the Soviet bloc as part of a larger world. Collins based his predictions on the long-term regularities of military geopolitics. Wallerstein focused on the dimensions of capitalist world-economy and political options accessible to the elites across its various zones. These are different but analytically meshing dimensions. In fact, the combination of two approaches best explains the structural factors of China's lucky exit from communism.

History surely made a big difference in shaping the character and divergent outcomes of Russian and Chinese communisms. Economic historians have now amply documented the pioneering role of medieval China in fostering the nearly modern levels of manufacturing and trade. Imperial China, however, did not become the first capitalist power in history for mainly geopolitical reasons. It was primarily the impressive permanence of an empire concerned with maintaining internal "harmony" and preventing nomadic attacks. In the West after the fall of Rome such an empire failed to materialize, which forced western capitalists to protect and consolidate themselves first as a system of city-states and later as modern national states. The Chinese empire fell late in the nineteenth century, but this series of catastrophic events only harmed indigenous capitalism. The Chinese entrepreneurs now faced both internal disorders and foreign domination by Western powers and Japan. It took another century full of grievous turmoil before the communist rebels prevailed in China—and essentially got stuck there. The Maoist attempt to launch a Soviet-type industrialization at the expense of the peasantry backfired in a huge famine followed by the decade of political bashing within party ranks. The human catastrophe surpassed even that of the Soviets in the 1930s without, however, generating a large modern industry and urbanization. China remained incapable of reaching even its immediate objectives in the regional neighborhood let alone the ideological goals of promoting a world anticapitalist revolution.

Here the geopolitical theory of Randall Collins identified a blessing in disguise. China was firmly contained in the world and regional power balances. Yet the same fact also removed China from the battle lines of the Cold War, thus enabling ideological decompression and economic engagement with the West. The Chinese cadres regarded radical Maoism as no less threatening to themselves than the Soviet nomenklatura regarded Stalinism after 1953. The long historical tradition of China suggested then the restoration of internal "harmony" by permitting grassroots and mainly rural economic entrepreneurship. Luckily, it was still surviving in the wake of abortive Stalinist industrialization. China's market turn evidently also helped to keep in line the local party cadres through patronage that delivered opportunities for personal enrichment while exempting the loyal and properly performing clients from the public prosecution for corruption. Communism did not collapse in China. Even the official communist ideology still survives in a "lite" version. The Chinese leaders coming to the helm after Mao stumbled into the combination of structural conditions that reproduced on a grander scale the East Asia authoritarian model of the export-oriented developmental state. This realized the long-standing prediction of Immanuel Wallerstein: the communists rejoining world capitalism as pragmatic facilitators between foreign capital and their national labor.

CAPITALISM AND ITS TWENTIETH-CENTURY CHALLENGERS

Military geopolitics recurrently emerges in our analysis of communism because this appears the single most important factor determining the twentieth-century revolutions. To stress again, communism emerged not from the ideas of Karl Marx nor from the native traditions of Russia or China. It was the result of a particular leftist current, the Russian Bolsheviks, first finding its opportunity in the wake of a disastrous war to seize and technologically upgrade an eminently defensible platform in world geopolitics. The Bolsheviks, themselves consciously following the French Jacobin precedent, showed how radical intelligentsia could inspire and mobilize the popular masses for overthrowing old regimes, defeating foreign invasions, and building the stronger new states on much broader social bases.

The Soviet example, through direct aid or mainly by its very presence in the twentieth-century world scene, enabled the success of a whole variety of patriotic insurrections led by the radicalized native intelligentsias. Far from all became communist but surely all adopted some of the strategies pioneered by the Bolsheviks. The difference was mostly in the degree of economic expropriation by the newly reasserted states. Wherever states moved to control everything down to peasant households, the state was declared socialist. In states that seized only the properties of foreigners and some particularly "obscurantist" or unpatriotic owners, like the landlords and large comprador traders, the process and its result was called nationalism. The aftershocks of Bolshevik revolution emerged most strongly in the other erstwhile agrarian empires humiliated by Western capitalism and reduced to dependency status. This is what became known as the Third World national liberation movements, from the early example of Kemalist Turkey after 1918 and the Indian epic struggle for independence to the Iranian revolution of 1979. In the latter case a postmodern student movement of the 1968 type ignited a typically premodern rebellion of the urban poor and merchants against the impious despotism of the Shah. The result, however, was a quintessentially modern revolutionary state more closely resembling the Soviet-type regimes than the medieval Caliphate. Just as the two world wars in crucial ways defined the Soviet Union, the eccentric regime of the Islamic Republic was consolidated in the tremendous patriotic resistance of Iranians to the attack by Saddam's Iraq which was surely acting as proxy of a broad counterrevolutionary coalition of foreign interests.

Despite the farrago surrounding the Sunni jihadi militancy after 2001, in the big picture of antisystemic challenges it was only a minor aftershock overdramatized by the American blunder of invading Afghanistan and Iraq. Al Qaeda sought a global geopolitical confrontation by the terrorist provocation of "morally cleansing" revolts and antiforeign resistance. Their strategy harkens back not to the Bolsheviks but perhaps rather to the nineteenth-century Russian Narodniki who had, after all, pioneered suicide bombings. And even more than the erstwhile Russian terrorists, the jihadists have failed politically to ignite popular rebellions.

In the core capitalist states, however, communist parties ran into the formidable wealth of Western societies and established parliamentarianism which favored the moderate tactics of social democracy. In the interwar Italy, Spain, and above all Germany, communists were brutally checked by the fascists, a new kind of counter-revolutionary force mobilizing both the embattled state elites and chauvinism of the "common angry men." The fascist variety of antisystemic movements must be addressed seriously because it might yet reemerge in the wake of large crisis. After 1945 the Western Cold War ideology equated fascism with communism as the totalitarian twin evils. The convergence in the techniques of mass propaganda, industrial warfare, economic planning, and state control was real enough but these techniques became more widespread during the twentieth century than many people dared to recognize. In the words of historian Eric Hobsbawm, the age of mass war and economic depression forced all governments to govern. This trend encompassed the more benign social democratic regimes of Scandinavia and the liberal democracies of Anglo-America that have shared to certain degrees in the new techniques of economic planning and mass consumption as well as police surveillance. Or just pay attention to public architecture and the typically muscular iconography of the thirties.

The scale of actual and symbolic state violence, significant as it was at the human level, depended mainly to the differential in geopolitical position and the strength of internal revolutionary challenges flowing from it. The dominant classes of Anglo-American democracies felt less threatened than their counterparts in continental Europe and therefore less compelled to let the violent and despicable racists fight in the streets against leftist revolutionaries or attempt to capture "living spaces" in foreign conquests. When it came to confronting Hitler's ultramilitarism that threatened to finish capitalism not in a revolution but rather in a very bloody mess, the Anglo-American liberals readily allied with the communist counterforce. In a great but perfectly explicable irony of the twentieth century, the capitalist world-system was saved by the Soviet military industrialization resulting from a communist revolution.

Fascism and communism meant radical escalations unleashed by the cataclysmic experiences of the First World War in the two rival political currents of the nineteenth century, nationalism and socialism. Both ferociously fought each other for the overlapping mass constituencies in the rising lower classes of society: clerks, junior officers, intellectuals, workers, peasants. Both movements offered to their followers vastly enhanced self-prestige, empowerment, and the prospect of unprecedented promotions through the ranks of party, state bureaucracy, and the military. The two movements were breaking the taboos of old aristocratic regimes and advancing whomever they defined as their common men.

It is an uncomfortable realization that the modern ideal of justice and political rights for the common people, in theory and in practice, could have not one but two antagonistic expressions. Justice as social equality and unity of humanity was usually called socialism. It is, of course, the original Enlightenment ideal that enjoys a great intellectual tradition and enduring attraction. But at the level of politics this program was never easily sustained because it cuts across the social cleavages of group status, locality, religion, race, and gender. Justice in less universal terms, as privileging only a particular group against other groups, typically translates into the politics of nationalism, sexism, racism, religious fundamentalism, or whatever their contingent mixture. The intellectual tradition of such ideas is much cruder. But they often proved more effective in the age of mass politics. Nationalism over the last two centuries has animated a great many passionate or downright virulent political mobilizations. In fact, it is still the most effective of all political programs today.

Communism was not a genetic twin of fascism. They were ideological opposites and mortal enemies emerging from the imperialist industrial warfare of the early twentieth century. Neither communism nor fascism can re-emerge in their familiar forms because, fortunately, their geopolitical and ideological preconditions have been eliminated. It does not mean that another major crisis in the future will not provoke strong reactions from the opposite sides of political spectrum. In fact, such antagonistic reactions will become likely as the conventional political mainstream loses coherence. But if my co-authors in this volume are right in their future predictions, as they proved in the past, then we might also make several further predictions.

The crisis of capitalism in the 21st century will be unfolding primarily in the world economy rather than in geopolitics. Its consequences will look more like class struggle, broadly construed to include the educated specialists, than world wars among coalitions of states. Moreover, the struggles will involve primarily the core capitalist areas where democratic politics have strong institutions and the enduring traditions of social movements. At stake will be public control over the private economic corporations rather than state armies or ideological paramilitaries. The nasty xenophobic reactions will be still prominent on one side because class struggles in a global world full of migrants inescapably will acquire the aspects of race, religion, and ethnicity. Extreme nationalisms will likely attempt to direct the powers of modern states into extreme coercion and policing resembling the erstwhile totalitarian practices, perhaps taken to a new technological level. Here is a big danger. But on the other side we will see political coalitions mobilizing around the liberal-leftist program of universal justice that has been ascendant in the modern world since at least the epoch of Enlightenment. Both capitalist classes and social movements, learning their lessons after 1945, cumulatively did a lot to make far less likely the wars between states and the internal civil wars. If warfare could be avoided, then violent revolution and dictatorships of both far left and the far right might be also avoided in the twenty-first century.

If this analysis is correct, then the Bolshevik 1917, fortunately, is not very relevant in predicting what the end of capitalism will look like. It could be rather the mass civic mobilizations like the 1968 Prague Spring and the Soviet perestroika at its height in 1989. In both instances the ruling elites re-acted with more panic than outright violence. But the insurgent movements even more shamefully failed to exploit the momentous disorganization in the ranks of dominant classes. The outcomes were unhappy. Therefore thinking boldly and responsibly about the future should imply considering the political and economic programs as well as the possible coalitions and tradeoffs in order to minimize the uncertainties of transitions in the face of major crisis. Ultimately, this could be the most useful lesson of communism.

5

WHAT THREATENS CAPITALISM NOW?

Craig Calhoun

Capitalism appears to be surviving the worst financial and economic crisis since the Great Depression. Though its lows were not as low, in the world's rich countries this has brought a longer period of depressed or absent growth than the Depression itself. Moreover, the current crisis comes on the heels of a damaging era of lopsided financialization, neoliberal weakening of social institutions, and intensified inequality. This exacerbates problems, undercuts capacity to deal with them, and reduces the buffers that protect ordinary people from the effects of economics upheaval. Investors are still making money; no states have completely collapsed. Yet the future looks precarious.

However, this and most talk of collapse reflects views from the old core countries of the capitalist world-system as they lose their privileged and profitable position. The views are different from many places in Asia, Africa, and Latin America. The current crisis both reveals and accelerates a shift of economic momentum away from long-standing core economies in Europe and North America toward newly developing regions. A key question for the future of capitalism is whether this momentum can be sustained. Capitalism is being transformed through this West to East and North to South shift, perhaps in ways that restore its vitality. But the rapidly growing economies also face challenges. And renewed capitalist growth in the old "core" economies also depends on transformation, particularly in the relationship of capitalism to political power and social institutions. Crucially, capitalism is vulnerable not just to market upheavals, excessive risk-taking, or poorly managed banks but also to wars, environmental degradation and climate change, and crises of social solidarity and welfare.

To think well about how capitalism may face decline, or be renewed, or be transformed, we need to recognize that it is not a perfectly self-contained system. One may abstract from more complex historical conditions to examine a putatively pure capitalist system. But the lived reality of capitalism always involves articulation with noncapitalist economic activity and with political, social, and cultural factors; it is a legal and institutional as well as an economic system. And many of the deepest threats capitalism faces come from its dependence on factors beyond the purely economic.

I will argue against the notion that capitalist collapse is imminent, and suggest that if capitalism were to lose its dominant place in global economic affairs this would more likely come about through protracted transformation and the rise of other kinds of economic organization alongside continuing capitalist activity. But this doesn't mean capitalism's long-term future is assured.

First, there remain issues of systemic risk and the balance of finance with other economic sectors. Second, capitalist profitability often depends on externalizing the costs of its activities—human and ecological as well as financial. Issues like pollution or unemployment in volatile markets demand the attention of governments or other social institutions. There is a deficit of institutions to do this work; social development has lagged behind economic growth where capitalist growth is newly rapid, and neoliberalism has weakened the institutional capacities of Western countries and even created challenges for political legitimacy. Third, capitalism is vulnerable not only to "intra-economic" or institutional factors, but also to external issues like climate change or war. There are questions about the extent to which capitalism—that historically unparalleled machine for producing economic growth—is up against environmental limits to growth and potential geopolitical conflicts exacerbated by unequal growth.

In each of these areas, dealing with the threats to capitalism may transform it, not cause its collapse. Together, they may bring about a world in which capitalism remains enormously important and potentially recovers some of its vitality, but is no longer able to organize and dominate a world-system to the degree it has through recent history.

WHY NOT COLLAPSE?

The idea of capitalism simply collapsing—as, say, the Soviet Union collapsed—is a bit misleading. This implies suddenness, a transition over just a few years from existing to not existing. The Soviet Union could cease to exist almost overnight because it was a particular institutional structure—a state—and its legal form could be dissolved. But capitalism is not strictly analogous.

As a state, the U.S.S.R. was a kind of corporation, and it was in the first instance this corporation that dissolved. But of course the dissolution of this legal-political structure also brought wide-reaching changes in other relations of power and practical activity. Still, many institutions that had been knit together through the Soviet state continued to exist with varying degrees of change in its absence. The city of Moscow had a legal and institutional status in the Soviet Union and a not completely dissimilar one in the successor Russian federation and republic. Gazprom changed more. Its creation in 1989 restructured the legal status and operating organization of the preexisting Russian gas industry. After the dissolution of the U.S.S.R., Gazprom was privatized in 1992 and has since operated as a joint-stock company. It was subjected to asset-stripping in the 1990s, then partially re-integrated and brought under state control in the first decade of the 2000s. In similar fashion one could trace a long list of partial continuities and partial transformations.

Nonetheless, Derluguian's account of how the U.S.S.R. could be treated as stable and obviously enduring almost to the moment it reached its end is instructive. It is a mistake to view the future only in terms of linear projections without considering possible sharp discontinuities. Derluguian reminds us of how pressures can build up to make a system both hard to sustain and vulnerable to small actions and events that have large consequences because of the unstable integration of the whole. He reminds us also that even a large structure that has come to be taken for granted as providing the basic context and conditions for the rest of life can be much more mutable than its surface continuity suggests. But we should recognize that the Soviet Union was not equivalent to socialism and thereby somehow directly analogous to capitalism. It was something more particular and of a different order.

This is so whether we treat capitalism as a set of practices that can be undertaken by capitalists anywhere, or as an economic system that knits together enterprises, markets, investments, and labor throughout the world. Capitalism is a historical formation, grounded, as Michael Mann would say, in a set of power networks. It has existed for the last 400 years primarily in the form of the modern world-system that Immanuel Wallerstein has analyzed. This is a hierarchical and unequally integrated organization in which the primary units are nation-states and economic actors are crucially dependent on relations with and conditions provided by political power.

To be sure, the idea of a nation-state is in a sense aspirational; the suturing of sociocultural identity to governmental institutions is never perfect; economic integration can itself advance national integration and certainly economic actors also influence government. Yet even if partially a fiction, the nation-state is a crucial formal unit for participation in global affairs, reproduced in political isomorphism. Most international organizations are literally that—structured by nationally organized participation. And states organized in this way provide crucial underpinnings to capitalism. They provide the legal and monetary bases for both firms and markets. They manage, or provide settings for the management of interdependence among different firms, industries, and sectors. By organizing structures of cultural and social belonging, however imperfectly, and sometimes by regulating markets, they organize workforces, consumer markets, and trust. The term "nation-state" may be only shorthand for "efforts to organize politics and sociocultural belonging in terms of nation-states", but the era of capitalism and the era of nation-states have been one and the same. There is no "real" capitalism, no matter how global, that isn't conditioned by this political-economic and sociocultural organization. The import of this is that existing capitalist prosperity and sustainability depend on nation-states and institutional affordances they have provided. These must be renewed or replaced. Yet for forty years the OECD countries have turned away from this task. Instead they have hollowed out the "welfare state" institutions of the past, reducing costs and pursuing immediate competitiveness but neglecting the long-term well-being and security of their populations and the collective investment that enables future economic participation.

That said, most of the old capitalist countries of Europe or European settlement are not at the point of immediate collapse. Britain's National Health Service still works, though costs are rising and threaten national budgets. The United States has actually, very belatedly, improved health provision (particularly addressing the large number of people who do not get health benefits from their jobs). And so forth. There has been great erosion. National budgets are in deficit and do not allow for easy rebuilding. But it is not necessarily too late to get houses in order. A wakeup call comes from those European economies that face such dire fiscal crises that they can only cut support for their citizens—precisely at a moment when they need it urgently. Spain, Portugal, Ireland, Italy, Greece, and Cyprus have teetered on the brink and others may. But this threatens the European Union more than capitalism as such.

Capitalism could swing further and further out of equilibrium. This might represent the irreversible "bifurcation" of a quasi-natural system (as Wallerstein has it, following Prigogine); or the failures of regulation, corporate strategy and investor prudence in chaotic capital markets; or indeed simply weak institutional coordination among dispersed and differently interested actors. It could represent a failure to distribute wealth widely enough to create demand for enhanced productivity, one possible consequence of the decline in job creation Collins envisages (though the political consequences of unemployment may be more immediate). Whatever the underlying dynamics, loss of a stable equilibrium increases the costs of trying to hold capitalism together, heightens political strains, and produces social tensions. This kind of disequilibrium is one way of interpreting what crises mean, and the greater the disequilibrium the more difficult and expensive the action required to restore equilibrium.

Nonetheless, I think capitalism is not likely to collapse. It may lose some of its grip on the course of social change. It may organize less of social, economic, and political life. But the image of collapse is misleading. To say the Roman Empire collapsed is meaningful, but it is worth noting that it took over 200 years, not just a single crisis. To say feudalism collapsed and in the process gave birth to modern capitalism—the schema offered in *The Communist Manifesto*—is less realistic. First, feudalism was not "systemic" in quite the sense modern capitalism is. But second, there was no moment of the collapse of feudal relations or related institutions. The long decline in feudal relations came in an era of state-building and war, of agricultural innovation and growing global commerce, of religious revitalization and Reformation—and it lasted at least 300 years. It was not simply a collapse. The Catholic Church was deeply transformed during the era when feudalism declined, and never played the same role afterward, but it survived. Many monarchies disappeared, though not all; some managed transformations enough to remain—and sometimes remain significant—in an era that could hardly be called feudal.

The end of the capitalist era, if and when it comes, is likely to be comparably rough, uneven, and hard to discern in midprocess. There will be institutions that survive it, including quite possibly many business corporations, which needn't stop trading, manufacturing, or speculating just because capitalism stops being the driving force of the age. The effort to buy cheap and sell dear long predated capitalism and likely will last long after.

CAPITALISM IN GENERAL AND FINANCE-DOMINATED CAPITALISM IN PARTICULAR

Capitalism creates a variety of problems for itself, for human society, and for nature. But for the most part these problems don't drive capitalism into potentially fatal tailspins. Extreme financialization does produce such vulnerability.

Finance is of course a basic part of capitalism, providing it with dynamism, capacity for rapid expansion, and tools for managing costs over time. It has been crucial to technological revolutions. More generally, it is central to the basic, definitive ability to move capital from one investment to another based on anticipated greater profits.

As its name suggests, capitalism is centrally a way of organizing economic activity through the fluid deployment of wealth—capital—by means of investments in different kinds of profit-making enterprises. Capital is invested or investable wealth. Finance—including straightforward debt but also a range of tradable securities—is an important part of this, crucial to the liquidity and mobility of capital as well as to expansion and spreading costs over time. Entrepreneurial dynamism depends on financial backing. But lopsided financialization can be distorting in a variety of ways. It has brought dramatic increases in domestic income inequality in all the major capitalist economies; it has channeled funds away from investment in productive enterprises. It fueled a long "megabubble" in asset prices, including the more specific bubble in mortgage-backed housing prices that helped precipitate the 2008–2009 crisis. It encouraged speculation.

During the years before the 2008–2009 market crisis, trading in equities and debt overtook employment-generating and profit-sharing industries in the old core of the capitalist world-system. Where financial instruments accounted for only a quarter of invested assets in the 1970s, by 2008 financialization had brought the total to 75%. Globally, financial assets accounted for some four times the value of all equities and ten times total global GDP.

This was a global phenomenon, shaped by a range of factors largely dating from the 1970s and accelerating toward the end of the 20th century. Because of its unpopularity, the United States financed the last years of the Vietnam War largely on credit. Seeking to manage economic difficulties in the 1970s, the United States and other core capitalist countries brought the Bretton Woods monetary system to an end, replacing the stabilization of backing by precious metals with floating, infinitely tradable fiat currencies. After the 1973 Arab-Israeli war OPEC oil producers restricted supply, vastly multiplying their returns from a world deeply dependent on petroleum, and then channeled much of the money into sovereign wealth funds. But financialization was at its most extreme in the world's long-standing core capitalist economies (and weaker economies yoked to them, for example by membership in the European Union or asymmetrical commodity trade). And while it was led by big capital it also drew in ordinary citizens who saw their incomes stagnate but continued high levels of spending by relying on credit. A better balance between productive industrial enterprise and finance is in fact one of the advantages of today's higher-growth economies like China or India as they move from semiperiphery to core in global capitalism.

The recent financial crisis reveals the main internal vulnerability of capitalism. This is systemic risk—that is, risks embedded in the complex web of internal connections that make up the modern financial system. It is important to be clear about this and about the nature of the crisis. This was not a "classic" capitalist crisis of overproduction and underconsumption. While it had a wide range of impacts in the "real" economy of manufacturing and consumption, it was first and foremost a financial crisis. Its impact was multiplied by the enormous growth in global finance during the decades preceding, and especially the extent to which financial assets came to dominate, especially in advanced Western economies. It was this that made overleveraging, excessive risk-taking, poor or absent regulation, and the heavy use and abuse of a range of new financial technologies so dangerous and ultimately so damaging. Not only did financialization increase the scale of financial assets, thus increasing the impact of a financial crisis. In addition, and more basically, it increased the interconnection of capitalist institutions joined not only in more or less transparent market transactions but also in a host of complicated and often opaque financial relationships. This was particularly true of the financial industry. When major banks were described in 2008–2009 as "too big to fail" it might have been more accurate to say: "too connected to fail." But financialization did not only affect firms in the financial sector; it became a basic part of all large-scale global capitalism. Car companies became auto-finance companies. Mining companies were tied centrally to exchange-rate arbitrage.

Financialization enhances the dynamism of capitalism. It facilitates the "creative destruction" of existing structures of capital (e.g., specific modes of industrial production) and spurs the development of new technologies, products, production processes, and sites of production. When extreme, though, it drives investments toward ever more short-term profits and undercuts long-term and deeper growth. It also produces speculative bubbles and busts. It increases market pressure on firms bringing less than median returns to capital, driving disinvestment from still-profitable older businesses and thus driving down wages and reducing the tendency of industrial capitalism to share profits through rising wages. It intensifies inequality.

Financialization leads to returns on invested wealth that far outstrip returns on employment. It rewards traders more than material producers (and despite celebrated exceptions, far more than most entrepreneurs). It makes all other sorts of businesses pay more for financial services. The 2010 bonus pool for securities industry employees in New York City alone was $20.8 billion; the top twenty-five hedge fund managers earned $22.7 billion. And this was after the market meltdown revealed the damage financialization was doing to the larger economy.

While technological obsolescence and spatial reorganization are both general features of capitalist growth, they are accelerated by financialization. Financialization increases the rate at which investments move from old to new industries and old to new locations. The result of this is not only technological and economic change, but also human displacement. Rapid urbanization in developing countries and decaying industrial cities in older core countries are two sides of the same process. With declining profits in manufacturing, European and American companies in a range of industries responded by demanding that workers take cuts in compensation, introducing new technologies, insisting that governments provide tax breaks or outright subsidies, and/or relocating manufacturing to other countries. Sometimes relocation came even after corporations benefited from subsidies and wage cuts, in defiance of commitments to stay put. Neoliberal governments aided corporations in breaking the power of unions to resist these changes. This helped bring about the loss of good jobs that Collins sees as a long-term threat, but it is important to see that the reasons were not all technological. Financial capital enabled the rapid relocation of industrial production.

Fluid financial resources also fuel asset price bubbles. The long, international real estate boom of the late 20th century is an example. This brought dramatic housing price increases, especially in cities and tourist areas. This often added to economic imbalance and produced other distortions, but crucially it knit real estate and construction, the personal savings of home-owners and the once-prudent operations of local banks into a gigantic international system. It was this linkage that generated the systemic risk that led to crisis in 2008–2009.

This systemic risk was enhanced by new techniques in financial engineering and investment. Hedge funds and derivatives took on central economic roles, aided by failures of regulation. Basically this meant developing a host of new financial instruments, many of them knitting different economic actors together in a web of mutual obligations like debt and insurance, and attracting unprecedented amounts of money to those new sorts of investments while deploying this money in trades largely hidden from public view. A host of seemingly stable local assets—like home mortgages—were bundled into securities traded globally by investors unable to assess their underlying quality. Even though many of the new instruments were designed to reduce risk and make capitalism more predictable, they became objects of largely speculative trading. Risk became more concentrated and dangerous. It became harder for specific firms to know how much they were exposed and to whom.

Derivatives—essentially securities based on bets about the eventual price of an underlying asset—were used as insurance to offset other risky investments. They also became high-risk but potentially high-payoff investments, not least by hedge funds. By the 1990s, capital in such "alternative" investments had passed $50 trillion and it reached about $600 trillion by the 2008 crisis. This may have encouraged fund managers and other investors to believe risk had been tamed, but recurrent failures of hedging suggest otherwise. Sudden liquidity shortages and political actions could trigger massive failures. As Raghuran Rajan, former IMF chief economist, remarked in light of the Russian government debt default in 1998: "A hedged position can become unhedged at the worst time, inflicting substantial losses on those who mistakenly believe they are protected."

Completely eliminating these problems would end capitalism as we know it. We would no longer have capitalism if capital could not be moved among investments seeking greater return, and absent the demand for reinvestment in pursuit of greater productivity that drives innovation and accumulation. Regulation that attempted this would undercut dynamism and wealth creation. On the other hand, some level of regulation combined with well-organized government spending may be crucial to recovery and resilience. And economies with more widespread entrepreneurship may fare better than those that remain dominated by finance capital. In any case, it is sobering to consider that regulatory improvements since the financial crisis began have been minimal. Almost nothing has been done to reduce the potential for systemic risk.

Thinking from the Crisis

In March 2008 stock markets plummeted; retirement savings were wiped out. Major banks failed, especially in Britain and the United States. Other banks were judged "too big to fail" (in a process we now know to be partly a matter of insider-dealing between corporate executives and government officials). They were bailed out on a massive scale, turning public revenues not only into a compensation for excessive private risk-taking but also a direct source of private wealth. Some industrial companies were also kept alive by bailouts but by far the largest subsidies went to the finance industry where they were turned directly into capital without passing through the circuits of job creation or relief for homeowners struggling against foreclosure. Had governments not provided this support it is possible capitalist financial markets would have spiraled much further down, still more deeply damaging global capitalism.

The United States made enormous countercyclical investments both in infrastructure and in direct subsidies to the financial industry (yet possibly not as large as were required). Britain chose a program of fiscal austerity by imposing even more cutbacks on itself than credit markets demanded. And Europe's North—especially Germany—imposed austerity on its South, bringing the European Union near to a breaking point.

Continental Europeans thought their institutions had weathered the crisis better than those of Anglophones until the public finances of several EU member states began to collapse under strain. Banking bailouts, especially in southern Europe, turned the crisis of the private for-profit financial industry into a fiscal crisis of states. Greece, Ireland, Portugal and Spain all teetered on the brink of bankruptcy even after severe austerity programs had been imposed. Financial crisis exposed weaknesses in the very constitution of the EU and the eurozone—which were, in large part, products of the era of financialization. Intensified global competition seemed to call for a larger Europe to compete effectively with China and the United States—a logic not dissimilar to that which led Citigroup and the Royal Bank of Scotland in their rushes to expansion. The desire for a common currency—attractive to financial and business leaders in Europe—had led to its introduction without mechanisms for effective common financial governance or in general the political institutions to back it up. The European Central Bank was governed by a board representing different national governments with competing interests. Different countries pursued different fiscal policies and practices. And as the EU expanded beyond its original core states, European integration linked very disparate economies. Commitments to redistribution that were tacitly tolerated in years of growth became points of contention in the midst of crisis.

The futures of the Euro and the eurozone remain uncertain. Spain and Portugal have gained minimal stability only for Italy to wobble and Cypus enter a tailspin. No one knows how far the European crisis will spread: perhaps to old member Belgium or new member Slovenia, perhaps to the EU itself, endangering the very common currency agreement. Meanwhile, austerity programs seek macroeconomic rectitude by rolling back state provision of services and security. In varying combinations cutbacks were nationally self-imposed responses to market pressures, and the result of external imposition not unlike the structural adjustment policies the IMF demanded of debt-ridden Third World countries in the 1980s. States were harnessed to save investors from losses and global markets from deep depression. Though it was investors and the transnational financial industry that reaped the huge profits of the bubble era and most directly benefited from bailouts and government-provided liquidity, the crisis and remedial actions are discussed in terms of nation-states. Of course, trying to grasp all this as a matter of profligate Greeks and prudent Germans obscures the central role of financialization itself (and of course the construction of the financial crisis narrative in overwhelmingly national terms reinforces other aspects of nationalist ideology, including increasingly widespread xenophobia and especially Islamophobia). Profits made by financial institutions encouraged the European Union to expand and to turn a blind eye to fiscal problems in member states. Now the citizens of EU countries with stronger banks and balance sheets complain about having to bail out other nations, straining the European Union itself, and forgetting the extent to which the benefits of bailout went to the financial industry and those with large capital assets.

Even after massive infusions of taxpayers' money, European and American financial institutions remain shaky. Some had to take a "haircut" on loans made in high-risk markets; only intergovernmental finance has held off collapse. Almost all face a continuing effort to strengthen their balance sheets after ill-considered expansion during the bubble. But stock markets have regained their buoyancy, most recovering what they lost and some soaring to new highs. Initial public offerings are again producing profits (and again for a mixture of firms with serious products and profitability and those with little more than hopes and image). Investment banks and other firms have resumed paying big bonuses, thus renewing one of the incentives to excessive risk-taking (though more now pay bonuses in corporate stock and ban its immediate sale in order to tie employees' interests to the firm's wellbeing). But some are also laying off employees in recognition of "excess capacity"; fears of return to recession are serious. Regulatory reform has been minimal, leaving derivatives markets far from transparent and allowing massive leverage against modest assets. Banking is even more concentrated in a few giant firms than before the crisis. Housing prices remain low, and while rising in some places are falling again in others after seeming to stabilize. Credit remains tight; interest rates remain low and expected rises are feared.

The "real economy" remains depressed—if not quite "in depression." Growth in GDP is low; unemployment remains high; new job creation recurrently fails to meet analysts' expectations. Yet anxieties about inflation and government debt lead some to argue that the pursuit of growth must be foregone in favor of fiscal austerity. The long-term fiscal position of many US states is almost as bleak as that of Greece or Spain (despite short-term recovery in some), and though the federal government has fiscal tools states lack, it faces massive deficits without an agreement on a budget to cut or finance them in any combination. Economic discontent is a primary factor in widespread and deep political discontent. Populist anger at corrupt, self-serving, or incompetent government is linked to both more conventionally right-wing and left-wing ideologies. Weakened political legitimacy is a challenge to the continuity of capitalism.

But the developing European path seems to be neither collapse nor revolution but rather stagnation. Europe lacks growth, but still enjoys a relatively high standard of living and basically functional economic systems. There are goods in the shops (though more and more shops close). Most governments pay their bills (though they continue to cut expenditures). The dominant policy response has been austerity, the attempt to overcome deficits in state accounts. As this has had little positive effect, however prudent in the abstract and long term, politicians look more and more for growth but so far find few palatable mechanisms to produce it.

Having failed to address its financial problems as a Union, Europe faces a series of nationally structured financial crises. Yet there remain enough economic strength and political will in the EU to bail out banks and financial markets in each case. There is widespread popular discontent but so far no large-scale social movements challenging existing political parties or processes. Huge rallies and sometimes occupations in public squares signal the unhappiness but so far haven't found a way to turn this to new political programs rather than only objections to old. Right-wing populists have seized the moment with anti-immigrant and other reactionary programs, but even though they have seen ominous growth so far they remain fringe movements, their biggest effect being to pull mainstream conservative parties to the right. Europe's Left is barely visible unless one counts basically self-interested strikes and statist manifestoes in France. What has instead emerged is rather a series of essentially "antipolitical" movements, exemplified by Italy's Five Star movement under Beppe Grillo but echoed in other countries where citizens vote not for more effective government but against government and especially politicians. Popular response to economic crisis and weak government legitimacy has often included right wing and xeno-phobic agitations.

The United States tried more pro-growth stimulus and is being rewarded with modest economic improvement: perhaps 2% growth—vastly better than Europe's 0% to 1% but nothing to cheer about. United States prospects are improved at least temporarily by new energy resources and longer term by a more entrepreneurial economy. But the country's dynamism is under-cut by a deadlocked political process. While the Tea Party is now organized electorally mainly as a wing of the Republican Party, its roots are much more antipolitical—not unlike Italy's Five Star movement. Its legacy pulls the Republican Right not toward different solutions so much as a resistance to compromises and thus to all available political options. The Obama ad-ministration is mainly technocratic centrist, though making its major policy innovations on a handful of liberal issues. But it has been unable to bring about a major reorientation in the wake of the crisis. In finance the same organizations remain dominant and pursue agendas largely similar to before the crisis. Some of the biggest threats to the US economy lie in deficit-ridden state and municipal governments. Cost cutting at these levels reduces the impact of federal stimulus spending, but more basically state and local gov-ernments face long-term obligations that could spell fiscal collapse unless a combination of growth and inflation reduces the burden.

Though the roots of the 2008 crisis were centered in the United States and the European Union, its effects have been worldwide. The dense inter-connections and rapid flows of global capitalism and global media made it seem immediately obvious that the crisis was simply global. This was half fact and half illusion, or perhaps a distortion based on perspective. The roiling of capital markets did have far-flung effects. Plunging asset prices damaged sovereign wealth funds in Abu Dhabi and nearly bank-rupted its neighboring emirate, Dubai. Exacerbated unemployment—especially among youth—may have helped to spark the so-called Arab Spring (though clearly the economic crisis can be no more than part of a more complex story). Stock markets in Shanghai, Tokyo, and Johan-nesburg sank with those in New York and London, though they regained ground much faster. Factory workers in China and Vietnam were laid off with sagging global demand, though after faltering briefly the Chinese and Vietnamese economies kept growing. Prices for energy and other natural resources became extremely volatile. After first falling dramatically, they recovered on demand from still growing economies like China, then in some cases sagged again as the Chinese economy did the same.

For a time, even as the United States struggled to escape a double-dip recession and Europe struggled with the sovereign debt of several member states, China, India and several other developing countries maintained rapid growth. Indeed, Chinese policymakers' biggest concern through 2011 was not an economic downturn per se but rather "overheating," in which economic growth outstripped supplies of raw materials, labor, and other inputs and brought hard-to-harness inflation. Since China had become one of the biggest creditors of the United States, it (like other foreign investors) had to worry about the value of its dollar-denominated assets as well as about markets for its export goods. At writing, Chinese growth continues at a rate that would thrill Europeans, but growth has slowed rapidly, proving China is not immune from the global downturn. The overheated financial markets pose one challenge. Thousands of apartments sit empty in Beijing and Shanghai, bought by speculators hoping to sell them again quickly. If growth doesn't pick up soon, or worse, falls much below 5%, this real estate bubble could burst, bringing a downward spiral as overleveraged owners unload their holdings. This is a relatively local and contained example of systemic risk, but there are others on a much larger scale where highly leveraged financial markets are highly interconnected with each other. This is also one factor making China's leaders fear domestic discord.

In India, capitalism is comparably vital, more entrepreneurial, and less tied to central government. The last is a blessing, because central government is considerably less effective. India has more endemic poverty and a less developed infrastructure. Inefficiency is debilitating. But its growth has been substantial and it seems to face less threat from speculative bubbles. Like China, though, its economic and political efficiency is weakened by widespread corruption. And like China it faces widespread ecological-environmental problems (though not yet anything like China's air pollution disaster). More open to autonomous institutions, India has a more substantial range of philanthropic efforts to mitigate risk and alleviate poverty. But it faces massive inequality, and rapid urbanization presents this in newly challenging forms. State institutions to support those without the resources for market solutions remain modest.

Happily growth has also continued in much of Africa and in some of the emerging markets of Asia and Latin America. After years of being snubbed by the EU, Turkey now has a growth rate the envy of Europe though this doesn't eliminate public discontent. But many economies throughout the world are, at best, unsettled and global capitalist expansion is close to stalled. This exposes as illusion the notion that the BRICs and other emerging markets would simply carry on capitalist expansion without interruption—or in other words, that the crisis was entirely local to the world's richer economies. It was a global crisis and it is embedded in the globalization capitalism has helped to produce. That said, of course it did not have the same implications everywhere. The crisis speeded up the transfer of global economic power to China (and in varying degrees other "emerging" economies) that had begun as a dimension of the financialization of the world's richer industrial economies. Ironically, this closed the gap between rich and poor countries more than the prodevelopment policies and assistance of the earlier decades of industrial boom. Long-term growth has not made China immune to the global downturn, and other BRICs have seen much greater volatility (like Russia) or sharper slowdowns (like Brazil).

Still, the bottom line is that capitalism is not likely to end as a result of any economic crisis alone. It is the intersection of economic with political crises that threatens it most, or the erosion of the implicit bargain in which people accept damages to society or environment in the pursuit of growth. Europe raises the specter of no growth capitalism—almost a contradiction in terms—and it's not clear how it will cope. Asia seems still to offer growth, but in combination with volatile and vulnerable politics. And political unrest is recurrent, both where faltering growth brings disappointment to those with rising expectations and where elected leaders seek to diminish public freedoms and quash dissent.

Though the capitalist era has been shaped by the notion that an imagined pure economy could be sharply differentiated from state and civil society, capitalism itself has always been and must be produced in practices and organizations that cross those boundaries. The relationship between states and economic activity is constitutive, not incidental. Capitalism depends not only on the organization of markets as "objective" systemic phenomena but also on social and cultural constructions like the corporation—not just as a legal entity but as an organization of work. The expansion of capitalism has not only depended on states and societies, but on the exploitation of nature. In each of these three cases, capitalism is destructive of conditions on which capitalism depends—and extreme financialization and neoliberalism exacerbate this tendency. The future survival of capitalism depends on whether ways can be found to limit or reverse this destruction without eliminating capitalism.

INSTITUTIONAL DEFICITS

One can feel transformation and renewal underway in much of Asia and parts of Africa and Latin America. High growth rates make for widespread optimism about a capitalist future and even encourage governments to join activists in declaring commitments to "green growth" and the building of better social support systems. The contrast with austerity-plagued Europe and the politically deadlocked and only slightly faster growing United States is palpable. Yet there is a crucial similarity despite differences of mood and trajectory.

Capitalist growth has imposed enormous costs in pollution, social upheaval, and inequality. The appropriation of disproportionate wealth by a capitalist elite is manifest, even flaunted, though so far enough others have shared in development to mute protest. Corruption adds a further challenge on top of inequality. At the same time, huge investments in infrastructure and resources are demanded, both for industry itself and to house rapidly urbanizing populations. These costs are largely externalized, while the new wealth is appropriated by those able to own, command salaries from, or tax capitalist profits. That is, the environmental and social costs are not borne by charges on corporate balance sheets; moreover, governments pick up much of the bill for needed infrastructural investments.

So is it over with capitalism? It depends on an "externalization regime" that enables its enterprises to rely on states, nonprofit organizations, and indeed families and ordinary people generally to bear the costs of both enabling conditions like infrastructure and damages inflicted as byproducts of capitalist growth. Indeed, much of capitalism's profitability and growth depends on externalizing costs. Firms seldom pay in full for public investments from which they benefit—like health care, educating workers or building needed infrastructure. They produce pollution and waste but do not shoulder the financial, human, or natural costs of the damage. Capitalism generates terrific wealth, in other words, but it does it always with the byproduct of severe "illth" (to use the term coined by John Ruskin in polluted and poverty-stricken nineteenth-century England). It can continue to generate the wealth only as long as the illth is tolerated. States try to manage the tradeoff, but taxing capitalism adequately to pay for its own costs undercuts their international competitiveness and potentially eliminates capitalism's very wealth-generating dynamism.

Capitalist enterprises also derive a number of other benefits from states, ranging from defense of their property claims to opportunities to harness for private commercialization the products of government-funded research. States provide needed inputs from currencies to roads and security in such matters as contract law. Capitalism also depends on social solidarity and a range of institutions from schools to health care. These often provide opportunities to profit, even when they are partially organized on public or nonprofit bases. But more basically, they provide services that enterprises would otherwise need to internalize and a stable context for business.

Indeed, even business corporations are not altogether contained within or controlled by capitalism as an economic system; they are legally structured, enmeshed in politics, and do work for their members beyond the profits for their owners. Corporate employment has been a major source of welfare benefits including pensions and health care insurance, though this has been in decline during the era of extreme financialization, as companies subject to disinvestment or takeover bids lost ability to plan for the long term and pared expenses to make their profitability more immediate to please fickle financial markets. Even more important in mitigating life's risks—including those produced or intensified by capitalism—are governmental institutions from health to education to care for the aged and support for the unemployed. Many of these have been subjected to debilitating pressures during the era of financialization. At the same time, older institutions like family, community, and religious organizations are able to pick up only some of the additional burden. There are newly created nonprofit organizations founded both for self-help and as charities. For those with money to pay there are other approaches to managing risk, from insurance to savings. But as an economic system that inescapably produces risk and volatility capitalism depends on some structure of supporting institutions to help ordinary people cope. There has already been sharp erosion in socially organized mitigation of risks in long-standing capitalist economies and relatively slow development of new institutions for this purpose in emerging capitalist economies. This in turn raises questions about whether capitalism, and governments that support it, can sustain political legitimacy.

Capitalism has flourished, and secured widespread legitimacy, on the basis of institutions and social relations that have been damaged in recent decades; its renewal will depend on their renewal. This is partly a matter of providing for legitimacy, social solidarity, and social support. It is also a matter of dealing with the fact that capitalist growth is at the same time a matter of urbanization, resource demands, environmental degradation, migration, and a host of other issues—not simply investment, production and profit. The capacity to deal with these comes not just from markets but governments and indeed a wide range of social institutions. As Karl Polanyi argued in the midst of twentieth-century depression and war, looking back at the nineteenth century as well as forward, unbridled capitalist development always undermines the social conditions of its own survival as well as the greater good; efforts to build new institutional supports can both stabilize the capitalist system and underpin more effective sharing of the benefits of capitalist growth.

An implicit social contract underwrites the legitimacy not just of capitalist enterprise but also of the states that provide for its continuity: citizens tolerate inequality and the externalization of long-term costs in return for growth. Today's high-growth countries in Asia, Latin America, and Africa all face serious challenges producing balance enough in their growth patterns to maintain national cohesion and investment in the conditions of future growth. They will not obviously be able to sustain recent growth rates, especially in a low-growth global economy, and absent such growth they will face both bursting speculative bubbles and citizen discontent.

Europe and the United States face the same challenges without the benefit of optimism or growth. Anxiety about the long absence of economic growth and manifest political weakness dealing with this is palpable, but so far has not produced a social movement response capable of truly shaping the likely outcomes. Popular response to economic crisis and weak government legitimacy has come largely in right-wing and often xenophobic agitations. Government response in Europe is a debilitating effort to restore state fiscal balances by austerity programs while preserving the capital of those who were the primary beneficiaries of financialization and the precipitators of crisis. The United States has done more to stimulate renewed growth, but suffers from political deadlocks as well as the same determination that costs should be borne by taxpayers at large more than by financial institutions or their investors.

During eras of sustained and substantial growth, especially following the Second World War, capitalism generated employment and improving pay. At the same time, economic growth underwrote expansions in health care, education, transportation, and other benefits in which citizens widely shared on the basis of progressive taxation and government investments. Now citizens doubt their children will enjoy greater prosperity or opportunity than they do. The desire of citizens in rich countries to get richer is confronted by their countries' need to remain internationally competitive (not just for trade, but to command the allegiance of elites and corporations that may flee high tax regimes). There are good reasons to expect growth rates in the old rich capitalist core countries to lag global growth so that even if they remain rich, improvements will be reduced absent major structural reform. At the same time, institutional structures that long ensured the overall legitimacy of capitalism have been eroded since the 1970s and more sharply in the context of financial and fiscal crisis.

The term "neoliberalism" is used to refer to a package of policies that sought simultaneously to reduce government costs and active participation in economic activity and to reduce government regulation of capitalist markets. This post-1970s liberalism owed much to nineteenth-century liberalism. A central difference is that the later version sought to unravel a host of social protections and economic arrangements put in place as part of mature capitalism. Its major targets were institutional arrangements put in place in response to the Great Depression and in the long postwar boom. But the link to nineteenth-century liberalism is instructive, for it reminds us to recognize that the tension between pursuit of "unfettered" capitalism and the effort to compensate for capitalism's limits and excesses is an old one. In the nineteenth century, liberals often sought to dismantle traditional institutions that got in the way of capitalist profits as well as to limit new ones. And this is an issue throughout the developing world today.

In China, for example, the development of highly dynamic capitalism is in tension with long-standing local community structures as well as alternative institutions put in place during the communist era—like the *danwei*, which made a "work unit" the central provider of housing, health care, and employment (with certain similarities to paternalistic company towns in an earlier phase of Western capitalist development). Workers taking new jobs, especially those migrating to new jobs in fast-growing urban regions, are stripped of both older forms of social capital in their communities of origin and the institutional provisions once offered by the *danwei*. They make new ways of life in cities, doing well to the extent that they have money to purchase market substitutes for the older forms of provision and struggling more when they don't. Sometimes they create new social institutions for themselves, much as migrants to cities such as Shanghai a generation ago created native place and clanship associations. Often they live somewhat marginal existences, trying to save money either to send home or to bring families. The government attempts to regulate this process, for example using the *houkou* system to restrict unauthorized migrants' access to urban institutions like schools. The very existence of the restriction is evidence of the institutional deficit as much as a tool of social control.

As China develops further in a capitalist direction, however, it needs stronger institutions. The government is indeed expanding education and restructuring health care, not least through introducing a new system of primary care. There are anxieties about what institutions will provide care for the elderly in a rapidly aging society (with family provision undercut not just by changing attitudes but by labor migration and the one-child family policy). One may only speculate on what may develop to provide unemployment protection or social services. The new institutions could be charitable undertakings or mutual benefit societies, though so far the government has been reluctant to allow either much autonomy. It seems clearly to be following a capitalist path but it is unclear how much this will involve a replication of Western institutions, an emulation of the Western neoliberalism that tries to minimize such institutions, or some variety of state capitalism ("with Chinese characteristics").

State capitalism has been an exception during the last 450 years, but one possible transformation of capitalism would be for it to grow more common. Arguably Soviet communism already involved something like state capitalism. Certainly fascism did. Where governments today use reactionary nationalism to shore up their legitimacy, state capitalism seems more likely. The key point is that future capitalism need not be an extension of the "liberal capitalism" dominant in the last two centuries of Western history. The widely remarked link between capitalism and liberal democracy may turn out to have been only one way of relating capitalism to politics, shaped by particular historical conditions and struggles.

Of course domestic neoliberalism was closely related to the international promotion of "free trade." Reduction of tariffs and other trade regulation is in a sense similar to reducing restrictions on internal mobility and government efforts to shape markets. Providing military security (or advantage) and delivering social security converge with the perceived advantages of state-dominated capital investment and buffers against global markets to make it a plausible model. This is particularly likely in countries with little experience of liberal democracy. Of course, Western states have also run business ventures—especially in transportation, communication, and power industries—but these have seldom been organized for purposes of capital accumulation as distinct from compensating for market failures. It was a hallmark of neoliberalism to demand their privatization, and this has been extensive—not only in old core economies like Britain but in a number of developing countries, notably in Latin America. In any case, it remains an open question whether the characteristic institutional structure for capitalism moving forward will distinguish government, business institutions, and civil society from each other as sharply as has been the case in the West.

SCARCE RESOURCES AND DEGRADED NATURE

Continued capital accumulation is limited not only by capitalism's internal economic difficulties and problems in the reproduction of its social and political support systems, but also by destruction of its "natural" environment. Capitalism depends on raw materials, on the sustenance of a human population, and on the willingness of humans organized in different societies to tolerate the externalization of the costs of environmental degradation from corporate accounts to public ones—either in the form of government payments or socially distributed human suffering.

Addressing ecological and climate challenges is made harder by the ways in which "nature" has come to be understood. It has long been seen, especially but not only in the West, as the other to human society, often an obstacle to be overcome—thus obscuring the extent to which we too are natural beings and live only as a part of nature. More specific to the rise and flourishing of capitalism has been the construction of "nature" as *resources*. For capitalism, nature has existed to be used, exploited. Examples are familiar, from forests to water. Taking just the latter, global freshwater use tripled during the second half of the twentieth century (while population doubled). Technological advances let farmers and other water users pump groundwater from greater depths, potentially draining aquifers and lowering water tables. Building more and larger dams generated electrical power and sometimes controlled flooding, but it also displaced people, flooded farms, and killed fish. Rivers are literally running dry and lakes disappearing. Attempting to manage by price calculations almost always radically underestimates the costs contemporary use imposes on future generations.

Because nature-as-resources always appears limited and capitalism is organized as a system of perpetual expansion, capitalism also nurtures efforts to transcend the limits of nature. The combination of modern science with business and government backing has been remarkably productive of new technologies. These include engineered resources to augment natural ones, such as improvements in agriculture, new materials, and new ways of extracting energy. Capitalism thus has been basic to increased capacity to support human life, complementing "natural" potential with intensified agriculture based on fertilizers, mechanization, drainage and irrigation, and new crops produced on the basis of research. It has also brought science-based medicine with its own range of new technologies from pharmaceuticals to equipment-intensive hospitals. These have extended "natural" human life and also enabled more people to live full lifespans. New technologies also include production processes and equipment that vastly alter and largely reduce the role of living labor in creating new commodities. They include transportation and communication technologies that overcome obstacles of distance and geography, and other infrastructural technologies that make possible urban life on an unprecedented scale. Along with enormous infrastructural investments, these have allowed for dramatic expansion in human population, massive urbanization, and a huge increase in geographic mobility.

But the new organization of social life has also multiplied demands for energy, met especially by carbon sources from coal to petroleum but also by nuclear and other forms of power. New technologies have increased demand for a range of minerals. And not only does the great expansion in the scale of human life depend on scarce inputs, it comes with the cost of large-scale environmental damage, including potentially catastrophic climate change. The very intensification of agriculture that boosts food production commonly leads to soil erosion and other damage. Newly engineered materials are often less biodegradable. Carbon-based energy sources pollute. And a wide range of activities that expand with capitalist growth bring global warming. This is, indeed, one of the central reasons why from Rio to Kyoto to Doha it has proved so hard to find an international consensus supporting serious action on climate change.

More generally, in an era of financialization, efforts to tackle environmental degradation themselves become objects of trading. Proposals to manage polluting carbon emissions by carbon trading offer a prime example. Such "cap and trade" schemes mean setting a limit on emissions but letting those who don't pollute as much as that notional limit sell their alleged "savings" to polluters to allow them to pollute more. That such schemes gained traction owed more to the fact that rights to pollute could be profitably bundled into securities and traded by investment bankers than to their actual efficacy in reducing emissions.

The extent to which nature is used up or irretrievably damaged is a problem for the future of capitalism (as well as life generally). It is a problem that exceeds the categories of economic analysis. This is partly because natural resources are extremely hard to price appropriately (especially with attention to long-term sustainability). It is also because thinking of nature only as resources severely limits understanding of the true character of human participation in nature and dependence on the rest of nature.

Understood as essentially limited resources, nature is also an object of competitive appropriation among capitalist organizations and the states on which they depend. The politics and economics of petroleum have been the standout example of this for a hundred years, and especially since the 1970s. But a host of new competitions for scarce resources will shape the near future and pose challenges to capital as well as to states and human societies. Energy is basic. Minerals are needed for modern technologies. Water is in short and unpredictable supply and often polluted. Even agricultural farmland is an object of competition as arid Arabia and crowded China fight to acquire rights to fertile Africa.

Struggles over resources are also important among the potential provocations to geopolitical conflict. They are already basic to a range of mostly small-scale armed conflicts that straddle the boundaries of civil wars, interstate wars, and criminal activity. Meanwhile securing natural resources—both oil and a range of minerals—is centrally important to China as it grows. And securing these resources entangles China in relations with a far-flung range of countries including volatile but significant ones like the newly partitioned two Sudans, which sell most of their oil to China. Selling natural resources is crucial to Russia and some other parts of the former Soviet Union. Europe is a major importer from Russia, and has already been involved in conflicts over supplies on which it depends. Iran is an unpredictable power in the Middle East and in its wider influence on Muslim populations. The Gulf States are major international investors as significant players in the security of the region. If they become increasingly unstable, the repercussions will be major. Nigeria, long a prime example of the "resource curse," appears to have begun a more successful but still fraught path to development. Several Latin American countries are significant oil exporters and some, like Brazil, are also emerging powers. The United States has reduced its dependence on international energy sources partly by investments during the financial crisis, including new hydraulic fracturing technologies. New capacity to extract oil and gas from shale is perhaps the clearest example of a possible technological fix to one of the major threats to the future of capital accumulation (more so than "greener" technologies that so far have proved harder to scale up proportionately to energy demand). But the technological fix brings new environmental concerns. And capitalism remains deeply entangled in global energy and resource politics. The list of powerful countries so entangled could be extended. Energy joins with ideological commitments to sovereignty in disputes over islands in East Asia as in the politics of central Asia and even Britain's postcolonial feud with Argentina.

Energy resources are perhaps the most prominent factors making violent conflict more likely but not the only ones. Water and arable land are perhaps as scarce. And beyond resources there are tensions over religion, migration, borders, and quasi-imperial desires to expand territories—not to mention tensions simply over evidence that neighbors are stockpiling weapons or acquiring nuclear capacity. A variety of dictators and nonstate actors are additional sources of instability and potential sparks to ignite conflict. And actual conflicts of the last decade—especially the invasion of Iraq and lingering war in Afghanistan—have both exacerbated tensions and reduced the capacity of the United States to complement its hegemonic power by effective policing. All this makes war more likely in the future, and makes it more likely that small-scale or regional conflicts will become drawn into larger-scale geopolitical conflicts. In many ways the forty-five years of the Cold War appear as an interlude in a longer history of geopolitical conflict and restructuring.

THE INFORMAL SECTOR AND ILLICIT CAPITALISM

Together financialization and neoliberalism weakened a variety of institutions crucial to stabilizing capitalism in the relatively rich Western countries. These included not only state regulatory institutions but also trade unions and even corporations. Business corporations that had seemed to be stable frameworks for individual careers ceased to provide health care, pensions, and long-term job security; in many cases they ceased to exist as their assets were traded in capital markets, stripped of any obligations to employees, communities, or business counterparts. Communities were undermined by disruption of economic bases and population movements. Formal organizations provided less and less of a safety net to ordinary citizens, and indeed fewer opportunities as well. The transition was not as sharp a shock as the crisis of institutions attendant on the fall of the U.S.S.R. but it moved in the same direction. Religious organizations stepped in not just with charity but also with a range of institutional services from employment to counseling. And throughout the OECD countries, local networks emerged to organize partially noncash economies of mutual exchange.

Weak formal institutions are associated with growth in the informal sector. The term derives from the efforts (notably by Arthur Lewis and Keith Hart) to describe Third World settings where formal institutions had not developed on a national scale and as a result the formally recorded, monetary economy contained only a fraction of total economic activity. The rest, crucial to the actual survival of much of the population, involved in varying combinations reliance on "traditional" social relations repurposed to provide support in new circumstances, development of new alternatives for formal market relations such as barter, and networks of face-to-face relationships in which transactions could be conducted without regard to law or taxation. Some of the informal sector activities would be classed as criminal, others not. But though the concept originated in studies of the Third World, it is clear that an informal sector has always accompanied capitalism and the efforts of nation-states to organize legal frameworks to support and cope with it.

The informal sector has expanded dramatically during the last forty years. It is an important dimension of economic life in rich countries as well as poor, an important part of how people have coped with poor performance of public institutions (as in the latter years of communism and formally planned economies), and central to how people have dealt with declining provision of public goods (not least in posttransition formerly communist countries but also in capitalist countries imposing regimes of neoliberalism and austerity). Much of this is organized on a community level: small-scale barter, cooperative associations, cash trade that evades both taxes and the financial industry. The informal sector is not simply a site of social problems. It is also a setting for creativity. The garage-based inventors and entrepreneurs who form something of a Silicon Valley myth often organized their nascent businesses informally (at least in periods when venture capital was hard to come by). So do similar entrepreneurs in India and Nigeria today. And so do filmmakers and artists. The informal sector can appear sometimes as bohemian, sometimes surprisingly middle class. Its dynamic, attractive businesses may or may not pay taxes, however, and their workers may or may not have pensions or health insurance.

The informal sector is not just local community networks and other face-to-face alternatives to formal markets and formal institutions. It also has a large-scale dimension of transnational capitalist structures that operate at least partially outside state institutions and laws. The latter include money-laundering, banking, and investments backed up by force as well as contracts. They include tax-evasion, trafficking, and a range of illicit flows—from minerals (blood diamonds or coltan), to weapons (small arms mostly, but also tanks, aircraft, and missiles), to drugs, to people. This often illicit capitalism is often more formally organized than the name "informal sector" suggests, and it has revenues and investments running into many trillions of dollars (though not surprisingly hard to calculate precisely).

The already substantial industry of tax evasion and illicit investment flows was dramatically heightened by the manner in which communism was replaced by capitalism in Russia. To a very large extent this involved the theft of state assets by former state agents and their transformation into a mixture of capitalist enterprise with organized crime. This helped to give rise to massive illicit trade and poured huge new amounts of money into an already thriving global network of illicit markets. Perhaps a trillion dollars worth of unrecorded capital flowed quickly from countries like Russia to tax-shelters like Cyprus and the Cayman Islands, and then in turn was invested in legal as well as illegal businesses back in Russia and around the world.

The importance of both relatively local informal sector activity and large-scale illicit capitalism reveal weaknesses in formally recorded capitalist growth. In the first place, this growth is unable to accomplish distribution necessary to sustain social life and reproduction. Formal capitalism actually depends on the informal sector to maintain the basic conditions of life in many societies—and thus the social peace necessary for prosperity of the parts of societies based on legitimate markets. This is particularly true in the parts of capitalist societies most affected by formal market failures—in slums, for example, where residents must rely largely on each other and very small-scale entrepreneurship to survive because both large-scale capitalism and the state are ineffective. But it is also true sometimes on larger scales, where corruption testifies not just to individual greed but also to institutional underdevelopment. Secondly, the large amounts of capital drawn into illicit global trade both implicitly tax or siphon funds from the formal sector and make markets and risks less predictable. Of course, capital from the illicit sector may also find its way into legitimate capital markets and into direct investment in legitimate businesses (where it may or may not be accompanied by illegitimate management tactics—like bribery or threats of violence). Informalization and corruption undercut needed state regulation and integrate legitimate businesses directly or indirectly with illegitimate ones like drug or sex trafficking.

Much of the global political economy is organized in ways that exceed the "official" world-system of nation-states and capitalism. Collusion between states and corporations, organized crime on various scales, the political power of warlords and cartels that hold no political office, and the economic power of semiautonomous parts of states including militaries all reveal a more complicated world—and one threatening to capitalism as we know it. So do cybersecurity challenges from Wikileaks to hacking, malware, spear-phishing, and other tactics deployed sometimes with state backing and sometimes by freelancers, sometimes against states and sometimes against corporations. This is part of the transformation of capitalism, not all without historical precedent, but with an unclear future.

Conclusion

Though capitalism seems unlikely to collapse next week, it is also unlikely to last forever. It remains unwise to imagine the future only in terms of linear projections from the present.

Capitalism could be felled by internal contradictions, including its general propensity to crises and the specific intensification of risk that has accompanied lopsided financialization in much of the world. Indeed, surprisingly little has been done after the 2008–2009 market meltdown to improve regulation or market structures; the same firms and people remain largely in charge. The same risks are therefore still with us.

Equally important, though, are potentials for external disruption, whether from environmental catastrophes, diseases, wars, or rebellions. Infrastructural systems on which capitalism depends, like communications networks or energy supplies, could also be disrupted, possibly by political actors. For all these reasons, what has been a process of ever-tighter global integration may be partially reversed. Coping with disruptions may depend on more loosely coupled systems with different bases for resilience.

Capitalism could decline without collapsing, simply organizing less of economic activity as alternative systems organize more. Growth could slow. This could happen globally or, more likely, unevenly by country and region. The ever-tighter integration of global markets that capitalism has driven might be slowed or reversed, with differently organized systems in different settings. Capitalism might be more central to some of these, more hemmed in or marginal in others. Business firms, operating in close relationship to governments, could manage economic relations more, leaving less to "free" markets. They could be organized with more attention to goals other than capital accumulation. Social and political institutions might provide stronger or weaker counterbalances to capitalism; illicit capitalism could loom larger or smaller. Capitalism could thus remain a vital part of global political economy, but be less dominant. Or a radically new economic structure could develop.

The current crisis is not the first time that capitalism has survived only because states were willing to intervene and assume enormous costs created by capitalist "excesses." Of course, the citizens to whom these externalized costs are distributed are often unhappy. But if states aid capitalism by absorbing costs firms externalize, they also aid citizens by managing risks from unemployment to illness. So far there is little sign of social movements potentially able to topple states that impose austerity in order to defend capitalist financial institutions. This does remind us, though, that at least as important as capitalist vulnerability to crises is the likelihood that capitalism will be undermined by destruction of the political, social and environmental conditions on which it depends.

Meeting institutional deficits is a basic challenge. Of course the challenge can be met by nonstate institutions as well as states, particularly by nonprofit organizations but also sometimes by capitalist firms where they are stable enough to work as social institutions supporting their employees. Contemporary global capitalism is also buffered for many people by an informal sector that sustains populations poorly served by existing institutions but that also extends into large-scale corruption. A massive illicit sector mingles tax evasion with criminal enterprises. Both informal and illicit sectors are interdependent with more formal and legitimate capitalism. Yet they undermine institutions on which it depends, including states.

Whether states are able to continue providing operating conditions for capitalist growth is a serious question, as much in parts of Europe as in less developed countries more commonly associated with the phrase "fragile states." Fiscal crises complement security challenges. Infrastructural and other growth-oriented investments have been hard to deliver effectively. Regulating global finance and meeting environmental challenges call for effective large-scale, transnational governance structures, but efforts to create these are relatively weak. Holding together a global world-system depends on the hegemony and disproportionate contributions of some members. The United States' willingness to carry these burdens unilaterally is declining but neither a replacement nor a multilateral alternative has emerged. One possibility is that the world-system will lose cohesion in favor of competing regional structures—and capitalism may matter more in some than others.

Capitalism itself contributes to some of the "external" disruptions that may challenge its future growth—notably environmental degradation and climate change. There may be possibilities for "green growth" that will sustain capitalism and deal with the environmental challenge. Or there may be limits to growth that make capitalism itself problematic and unsustainable, simply because it is in the end a growth machine.

With regard to each sort of threat, there are actions to be taken that could counterbalance the damage and mitigate the risks of one-sided capitalist development. These could come from for-profit and nonprofit entrepreneurs as well as governments. They could be pursued by social movements—though so far none have risen to the scale of the global challenges. In any case, capitalism cannot thrive if institutions are not reshaped, employment restored, and environmental, public health, and other challenges addressed.

The large-scale, more or less simultaneous collapse of capitalist markets would be catastrophic, not only bringing economic upheaval but also upending political and social institutions. It could be precipitated by systemic crises or more likely brought about by ecological change or violence. The risk is heightened by capitalist externalization of costs and damage both to the environment and to potentially stabilizing social institutions. But discontinuous changes are not always sudden or catastrophic.

As I began by suggesting, it is at least as likely that capitalism will be transformed over generations, possibly beyond recognition. Arguably stronger states, better agricultural productivity, and renewal of religious faith were all solutions to problems in feudal Europe. They also transformed it and in the long run brought a new era. The rise of both state risk management and economic facilitation and capitalist corporations offered solutions to problems in mid-20th century capitalism. These were transformative, though contained in a still-capitalist order.

That capitalist order is a very large-scale, highly complex system. The events of the last forty years have deeply disrupted the institutions that kept capitalism relatively well organized through the postwar period. Efforts to repair or replace these will change the system, just as new technologies and new business or financial practices may. Even a successful renewal of capitalism will transform it and the modern world-system within which it has driven growth for 400 years. If nothing else, capitalism will be transformed by the extent to which growth is led from outside its long-standing Western core regions and this will integrate it with different histories, cultures, and social institutions.

The question is whether change will be adequate to manage systemic risks and fend off external threats. And if not, will there be widespread devastation before a new order emerges?

GETTING REAL

The Concluding Collective Chapter

Immanuel Wallerstein, Randall Collins, Michael Mann,
Georgi Derluguian, and Craig Calhoun

In the end, where do we agree or disagree? We share in common the assessment of our present world situation—including its intellectual and political climate—where we identify the blind spots and therefore the dangers of screwing up in the future. These agreements make up the main body of our concluding statement. But we are not hiding our theoretical differences regarding the ways in which we construe the world and its future prospects. In getting together to write this book, the immediate hope was that our unity as well as our differences would provide for a panoramic vision and a productive debate. The greater hope was that, if we succeeded in getting the attention of sufficiently many readers, we could also make a difference.

We agree that the world has entered a stormy and murky historical period which will last several decades. Big historical structures take time to shift or unravel. The recent Great Recession forces us all to think deeply about world prospects. The central question is not just the prospects for continued

American economic dominance and geopolitical hegemony, nor where on the globe such dominance will pass to next, but whether major structural transformation is likely to happen. Although we disagree on some points of the prognosis, there is considerable commonality in our sociological vision. All of us are arguing on the basis of the accumulated scholarship in the realm of macrohistorical sociology—the comparative study of past and present broadly informed by Marxian and Weberian traditions focusing on the structures of social power and conflicts. We are sensitive to multiple dimensions of causality, and tend to agree on many features of how capitalism, state politics, military geopolitics, and ideology operate. Our disagreements are largely about the intersections of different orders of causality: on whether a particular dynamic sector can become so powerful as to overwhelm the other causal spheres, or whether the multicausal world always generates a high degree of unpredictability; and on whether an overarching perspective can display a higher-order system bringing together all the causal sectors into a larger historical pattern.

In this concluding chapter we will first outline the macrosociological way of describing current globalization, its origins and possible futures. The latter part of our conclusion is about social science in its mostly deadlocked present state and its potential for becoming more useful in the immediate future. In other words, we are going to sketch here what we all consider a more realistic picture of the world and the ways of arguing about it.

The Making of Our Present

The (so far) Western Great Recession marks the end of the medium-run historical phase that began some forty years earlier, in the crisis of the 1970s. This recent period was confusing enough, as evidenced by a multiplication of misnomers: neoliberal, postindustrial, post-Fordist, post-Cold War, postmodern, postconsumerist, etc. Since the late 1980s, globalization has become the most fashionable generic description of the current world situation. All these names seem to us problematic. Globalization is presented as the grand historical cause of what really were the geoeconomic consequences of the 1970s crisis and subsequent shifts in the world allocation of production processes, or simply what came to be called outsourcing. These labeling dilemmas, however, relate to the fact that the current phase in the long historical trajectory of capitalism has lacked coherence or true novelty.

Even the arrival of the Internet, as Randall Collins argues, has revived the old dilemmas of machines displacing human labor and livelihoods. The major condition of the period from the 1970s to the 2000s period was not the emergence of any new structuring forces but rather the undoing of former ones. We mean primarily the exhaustion or extinction of all three Old Left currents: the social democrat and liberal reformism in the "First World" of core Western states; the communist revolutionary dictatorships of rapid industrial development in the "Second World"; and the national populist movements in the Third World.

The past triumphs of the Old Left had flowed directly from the geopolitical upheavals of the twentieth century: not from the abstract march of progress or even the growth of class consciousness per se but directly from the dire experiences of world wars and mobilizations on the homefront that gave opportunity to the peoples, both White and non-White, men and women. In this book Immanuel Wallerstein and Michael Mann, in their own ways, sketch the general lines of this transformation within capitalism, while Georgi Derluguian shows in greater detail what enabled the rise of the communist states and what processes and forces produced their divergent outcomes. The two world wars enormously boosted the long-running trend toward more extensive and invasive modern states. After 1917, in many countries leftist forces suddenly found themselves in a position to capture the wartime state machinery and redeploy its capacities for industrial growth and social redistribution. The intervening Great Depression in the 1930s opened to leftists—but also to fascists—windows of political opportunity by severely discrediting and bankrupting the residual aristocratic monarchies, the oligarchic liberal regimes and their colonial empires of nineteenth-century vintage. The Cold War after 1945 stabilized the results of this epochal transformation for several more decades. The Cold War (another misnomer, actually meaning the "cold peace" of multiple truces and implied diplomatic understandings) institutionalized the internal reformist compromise and welfare provision in the Western democracies, thus containing the specter of revolution long haunting the West. The same Cold War ensured peaceful coexistence with the Soviet bloc, thus containing the old Western specter of war. And by extending international political patronage and economic aid to the former colonies, the Cold War world order channeled the specter of anti-White revolt of colonial peoples into the optimistic and cooperative expectations of universal modernization. Those were the good times of generous payoffs for the trials and sacrifices of wartime decades.

The good times suddenly crashed in the 1970s. Craig Calhoun reminds us that the sequence of another political transition did not start from the resurgent Right. Rather, it was the youthful New Left that first challenged Cold War compromises by demanding still better times minus the official hypocrisies and sclerotic bureaucratism. True, contemporary establishments everywhere—West, East, and South—were showing many signs of bureaucratic pathology and despotism disguised with hypocrisy. Importantly, however, those detested establishments by the 1970s represented later stages of the various political regimes originating in the modernizing, socially reformist, anticolonial, or revolutionary takeovers of the earlier heroic epoch. For all the loudly proclaimed ideological differences, the wartime generation of states held in common their reliance on what the Americans called the triad of Big Government, Big Unions, and Big Business, or their functional equivalents in the Soviet industrial ministries and national republics. All these political and economic structures drew their power and legitimacy from the mass provision of modern education, housing, health and welfare services; typically lifelong industrial employment; and, not least of all, comfortable middle-class careers in the bureaucratic, military, and professional hierarchies.

Certainly many powerless social groups and peoples in different countries felt excluded from this bureaucratically organized prosperity. Typically, these were the racial, religious, immigrant, and gender minorities in the developed countries; the non-Russians and subproletarians in the Soviet republics; and the masses of recent rural arrivals in the sprawling shantytowns of the Third World. But such marginalized groups could rarely raise a political voice. Things would change, however, in the 1960s with the arrival of energetic student activists and dissidents in the intelligentsia spreading organizational techniques along with the ideologies and singable slogans of rebellion against "the System."

The antisystemic movements of the New Left gained traction wherever they could tap (often without fully realizing it) into latent social tensions generated by conjunctures of many factors: industrial recessions, demographic transitions, the changing social geography of urban neighborhoods, repressed ethnic memories, even the sectarian religious fervors or the regional elite factionalisms previously marginalized by modernistic planners of new towns, industries, and states. Profoundly changing the historical pattern of revolutions, these anti-authority rebellions were diffuse, non-violent in their preferred tactics, and centered on the demands for greater autonomy from bureaucratic regimentation and recognition for the many and greatly varied status groups that were now called identity politics. This meant a departure from the Marxian categories of economic classes as the basis of social struggle. What gave a semblance of common purpose to the disparate protests of the sixties was the universal presence of bureaucratic establishments, oftentimes presided over by the paternalistic and patronizing Big Bosses. For a short while, such situations were conducive to the sharply polarized confrontations of "us against them" performed in public spaces and on spectacularly massive scales. Recall the events of 1968 in the West, the tremendous anti-Shah marches in Iran during 1978–1979, the 1980 strikes in Poland and the 1989 rallies across the whole Soviet bloc, or, for that matter, the 2011 uprising against the Big Boss in Egypt.

The participants, commentators, and sympathetic researchers of these exuberant events focused overwhelmingly on the contentious side where all the energy and hope could be found. Contemporary analyses from the insurgent side typically ignored or took for granted what the embattled rulers were doing or actually not doing. In the majority of instances, bureaucratic establishments seemed oddly reluctant to unleash an all-out terroristic repression. This should seem quite startling because both "capitalist pigs" and "communist apparatchiks" certainly possessed the means and personnel for launching massive violence against unruly civilians in the manner of the interwar totalitarian decades. Grim exceptions still abounded in the stormy aftermath of 1968. We must not forget the brief throwbacks to European fascism that continued in Spain, Greece, and Turkey; Latin American dictatorships; the apartheid-era South Africa; coups and "emergencies" in Arab countries; and internal violence in the East Asian states of both communist and anticommunist persuasion, like Maoist China and South Korea under military rule. The immediate reasons for unleashing state terror in response to student-led activism were local and peculiar to each instance. Yet repression commonly occurred across the outlier world regions and semi-peripheral countries where states were inherently weaker and often newly established.

This contrast in the state reactions to protest points toward an important theory. In the West and in the Soviet bloc—but not in Latin America,

Middle East, or East Asia—the political establishments by the 1970s had indeed become thoroughly bureaucratic. Their institutions and ruling personnel were forged in the enormous wartime mobilizations of the twentieth century and disciplined by the precarious balance of the Cold War. Their senior members still collectively remembered the run-away affair with fascist paramilitaries during the interwar period in Europe, or Stalinist purges, or the racial and labor conflict violence recurrently flaring up in twentieth-century America. Perhaps it was the overwhelmingly peaceful and civic tactics of New Left, in contrast to the revolutionary militias of Old Left, that denied the state security organs clear targets for violent confrontation. Perhaps the bureaucrats and politicians ensconced in highly institutionalized environments developed cautious dispositions that were conductive to avoidance of overt conflicts. Instead such "post-Machiavellian" rulers reckoned on the default bureaucratic tactic of muddling through. And this suggests an important and even hopeful insight. Leaping ahead, we should say that studying the conditions for violent action and its avoidance in modern bureaucratic states must be a priority for social science in the anticipation of bigger crises and possible revolutions.

In the seventies and eighties, establishmentarian politics of muddling through and evasion delivered a fix that has lasted until yesterday. The New Left movements flared up and burned out as fast as fireworks. But the damage was considerable, especially when viewed in the longer-run perspective. The discredited and momentarily disoriented rulers began shedding their erstwhile commitments to industrial modernization, full employment, and welfare. In the West political systems had enough strength and resources to do this in a controlled manner, all the while calling it a new age of postindustrialism, flexibility, and globalization. In the Soviet bloc the process got out of hand, causing panic in the political and industrial elites. The result was state fragmentation and colossal pillage. The dissident New Left had its Pyrrhic victory in the extinction of communism. But, unlike the Old Left which was an organized (more precisely, a bureaucratically organized) force, the insurgent energies of this new generation failed to translate into institutions and policies adequate to the tasks of seizing the power that was dropped on the floor. Moreover, the ensuing deindustrialization, and severe budget cuts in higher education, cultural institutions, and general welfare rapidly undid the bases of popular confidence and thus the bases of support for this new generation of antisystemic insurgents.

In the meantime a different kind of popular movement began emerging from the Right. The New Right snatched many of its tactics and even former activists from the dispirited New Left. This turn to the right marked the end of the long period dominated by class politics with its familiar symbols, tactics, and well-rehearsed rituals of bargaining. The political reaction flew the colors of identity, which introduced into politics a nastily passionate charge because matters of identity tend to be uncompromising and nonnegotiable. The New Right came in two varieties, though often meshing in practice: ethnopatriotic or religious-patriotic fundamentalism and libertarian market fundamentalism. Both called for the militant defense of fundamental matters of faith—or whatever was claimed to be the founding identities in their societies. Notice that both fundamentalisms directed their ire at state bureaucracies, blaming them for being too secular, removed, devious and taxing. It tells us something important about Christian, Muslim, Jewish, Buddhist, Hindu and other contemporary fundamentalisms that their suspicions and phobias virtually everywhere went hand-in-hand with extolling the virtues of small business, small town life, and the patriarchal family.

The Left was precipitously declining across the board, leaving its place in the popular imagination to be filled with either apathy or fundamentalist anger. This reversal in mass politics opened the window of opportunity for conservative factions among the Western capitalist elites. Neoliberalism, yet another misnomer, in fact grows from the old ideological belief of modern capitalists that everyone would eventually benefit from letting them do whatever they deem necessary in the pursuit and disposal of profits. World progress, the purported laws of human nature, and supreme rationality are but the nineteenth-century intellectual supports to this faith. The fundamentalist character of the neoliberal movement is revealed in its adamant refusal to recognize as capitalism anything except the purest unregulated markets—just as religious fundamentalists recognize only their own radical brand of faith as true religion. History, however, shows that the ideal type of free markets cannot be observed in any empirical situation; it is an ideological fantasy. Following in the footsteps of Fernand Braudel and Joseph Schumpeter, we argue that sustained profits always require a degree of state protection and market monopoly. Hegemonic monopoly is what in fact propelled the renewed surge of American power and finance at the turn of the twenty-first century. At the time Michael Mann and Immanuel Wallerstein publicly opposed the project for an American world empire, and both presented analytical arguments questioning its viability.[1] There is now enough hard evidence to see how these predictions squared with reality.

The forty-year period now ending falls into roughly equal parts. The decades of the 1970s and the 1980s were marked by the crisis and collapse of the twentieth-century Left projects along with the political and economic structures of state-led national developmentalism. In the following twenty years, bracketed by the symbolic dates of 1989 and 2008, the American power found itself freed from the external pressures of the Cold War and the internal constraints of social compromises. The booming enterprise of neoconservative commentaries propagated a bullish belief in the return to capitalist normalcy while presenting it as the new, endless epoch of globalization. The post-1989 triumphalism referred in fact to the kind of normalcy experienced before the year 1914 (not the 1950s, which, although often conservative, were shaped by increasingly strong states). Back in the epoch of fledgling leftist movements and conquered non-Western peoples, capitalists could pursue their goals largely unconstrained by the demands of national governments, the considerations of social policy, and, for the first time, in a truly global arena that was unified by new transportation technologies and secured by military and political structures of colonial domination.

The prospects of twenty-first century globalization appeared to its advocates even brighter. American hegemony now kept firmly in check the imperialist rivalries of the kind that had finished off the previous globalization in 1914. The outsourcing of labor-intensive production from the core of the world economy to cheaper "emergent" locales in the periphery subverted national labor and environmental regulations and pressed governments and their citizenries to become "globally competitive." The dismantling of government regulations allowed the leading capitalist groups to focus on reaping superprofits from the devilishly complex games of global finance. Even popular revolutions, in a paradoxical return to nineteenth-century liberalism, turned from the nemesis of capitalism into its democratic promoters in previously closed countries. The capitalist-compliant democratizations were facilitated by a spate of nongovernmental organizations enthusiastically assuming the role of latter-day global missionaries. The politically and financially cumbersome colonialism of yesteryear was replaced in the newest era

---

[1] Michael Mann, *Incoherent Empire*. (London: Verso, 2003); Immanuel Wallerstein, *The Decline of American Power*. (New York: New Press, 2003).

of globalization by the indirect controls of powerful institutions of debt and the global network of American military bases, as well as the softer power of international advising, global mass media, and shared norms inculcated in the younger peripheral elites by acquiring prestigious diplomas in business and government administration from American universities. To this list of novel disciplining institutions, we should add illicit opportunities for money laundering through the global archipelago of microjurisdictions functioning as tax havens. The few remaining noncompliant and intransigent "rogue states" could be relegated to the Axis of Evil and serve a useful ideological function as the atrocious other.

These splendid designs ran into the structural realities of the world-system that had been profoundly transformed during the twentieth century. There could be no return to the pre-1914 imperial normalcy. Even the unprecedented concentration of military force in a single superpower in the modern age could not deliver on its geopolitical goals. In our own day the cruel coercive practices of past empires were bound to backfire. Perhaps the American jailers at the Abu Ghraib prison in Iraq stayed short of the methods of the Gestapo or, for that matter, Saddam's own torturers. Nevertheless, these shameful images when publicized produced a storm of nationalist indignation across the Middle East and revulsion in the West. Such episodes, along with the post-1968 aversion of Western societies to casualties among their own military, put political constraints on the use of violence. Add here the sheer material costs of logistical overstretch that have not declined in the era of military high technology but have even increased; in effect, American campaigns of foreign policing became exceedingly costly and politically impossible to win.

Immanuel Wallerstein identified a different kind of constraint to American hegemony and its neoconservative globalization. Despite the persistent rhetoric of tax cuts and downsizing the government, the actual levels of taxation have remained roughly at the same historically high levels virtually everywhere. But wait, what about the stories of budget crises, cuts in public employment, shrinking pensions, and woefully underfunded education and social services? Behind this paradox we discover the reality of the continued redistribution of surpluses through state channels, official or not. Redistribution was now running in the upward direction, to people located in more powerful states and overwhelmingly to elites making political and financial decisions. The result was a huge accumulation of wealth in the hands of those who effectively became the oligarchs of our times. It is fairly simple to see how they did it. The cuts in social redistribution (in a broad sense, including policies of industrial growth and employment) freed the money still flowing through the gigantic state machineries and channeled it to the financial oligarchies. This could take the scandalous form of bailouts extended to corporations ostensibly too big to fail, yet in the main it was the endless generation of credit which in recent decades had been extensively used to cover the budget shortfalls of states and individual families.

Here comes the rub. The reason why governments and families had to be provided with ample credits is both nefarious (yes, greed and debt bondage) and clearly vital to capitalism. In the more distant past, capitalism was an elite operation catering to the fabulous consumption of higher classes and the expensive wars waged by states. In twentieth century capitalism, for the sake of large-scale market demand as well as political legitimacy, came to rely on popular mass consumption. Moreover, the twentieth-century experience of popular involvement in politics and reliance on the state set limits to how deep human misery could go without producing a disruptive backlash. This proved to be what is called the "ratchet effect" in the historical tendencies of the growing state functions in modern society.

Democratization has been a real, if not inexorable trend over the past two hundred years. This means that a great many people, including those most loyal to the existing order, came to expect three things in the course of their lives. The first is long years of education, the second is stable and reasonably rewarding employment, and, finally, pensions in older age. Housing could be added to this list of expectations, and efforts to provide housing have also been expensive. The widespread privatizations of housing in recent decades shifted financial burdens to the individual homeowners while transforming them into small capitalists who voted accordingly. But this shift inevitably led to ballooning mortgages while denying the prospect of home ownership to younger generations. The 2008 crash in the housing markets of many countries rendered this contradiction untenable.

States, on their side, needed skilled and reasonably healthy citizenry as workers, compliant taxpayers, and patriotic military recruits. In time, these historical trends would inescapably put pressure on private profits. Western capitalists responded to pressure with their own rebellion. The renewed market conservatism became its ideological platform and market globalization its main strategy. The political-economic ideology of New Right demanded that capitalists, through deregulation and government austerity, should be left to deal by their preferred means with the economic upheavals that began in the 1970s and never really abated. Globalization, first and foremost, meant the flight of large capital beyond the regulated confines of national states. Capital flight and pressures on tax revenues left the majority of governments with three unappetizing choices: printing money, going into debt, or unleashing repression by direct police brutality and slower economic suffocation. Each of the choices was fraught with its own dilemmas. Even repressing the poor, marginal, and rebellious required a lot of money to keep the loyalty of those morally consenting to repression and especially those actually doing it. But where would the governments get the money when so much of their financial flows were already committed to oligarchic interests?

Such were the main political and economic parameters of recent decades. If anything, the same dilemmas are bound to get worse in the short to medium run. Wallerstein's theory of self-limiting capitalist aggrandizement thus parallels Mann's argument on the present-day limits to geopolitical aggrandizement. In the absence of organized and effective opposition, the accumulation of financial resources at one pole can reach exorbitant proportions. But just as the military monopoly of the United States could not be exploited anywhere near its full potential in order to reach its imperial objectives, so the financial monopoly inevitably had to falter at some point like a house of cards. The accumulated sums of nominal money could not be used productively and thus were proven fictitious.

This big picture relates mostly to the West and former Soviet bloc. Would it change substantially if we bring in the rest? Of course, the miracle of China looms here very large. Some of us, however, are old enough to remember the times when the experts in economic development were generally dismissive of East Asia's prospects. Their rising stars were rather the Philippines, the Shah's Iran, or Nigeria and Senegal with their Western-modeled institutions, modern infrastructure, sizable domestic markets, educated technocrats, and middle classes. By contrast, the embattled "garrison states" of South Korea and Taiwan or the relic *porto franco* colonies of Singapore and Hong Kong were found lacking in almost everything: national sovereignty, middle classes, natural resources, and modern education. The East Asian states seemed to contemporary experts weighed down by overpopulation, destitute refugees, endemic cronyism and corruption, and other such allegedly immobile Asian traditions. Communist China, with its mad Maoist experiments and fanatical guerrilla cadres, was dismissed outright, virtually like North Korea now. Ironically, the same factors would be later cited as standard explanations for East Asia's success: its abundant cheap labor, the shallow domestic markets suggesting openness to export opportunities, the fortuitous absence of a "resource curse" like oil, and moreover the same Asian values of discipline, hard work, support networks, and obedience to authority. Even these regimes' authoritarianism somehow turned out to be stabilizing, or adaptable and even visionary, rather than cronyist and corrupt.

Randall Collins in his earlier research pointed to the indigenous medieval origins of East Asian capitalism growing from the organizational economies of Buddhist monasticism.[2] It is now firmly established that East Asia for a thousand years or more has been a world region or world-system of its own, boasting some of the most extensive and dynamic markets of the epoch. The inherited skills, assets, and social networks of East Asia reemerged during the twentieth century in a variety of contingent and often violent pathways. It was the expansion of Japanese imperialism prior to 1945, and later the American wars to contain communism, that fostered in their wake a series of developmentalist dictatorships. Georgi Derluguian shows that the ultimate joining of continental China into this export-oriented capitalist dynamic was occasioned essentially by the conjuncture of international and domestic political accidents, albeit the sort of accidents that were structurally waiting to happen.

Free-market ideologists seek to enlist recent East Asian examples as their major proof of unfettered markets eliciting a wonderful burst of entrepreneurship. Such claims lack historical analysis and empirical evidence. East Asia has long been the prime example of regulated corporatist states. If the policies of neoliberal deregulation had anything to do with the reemergence of East Asia, it was by draining even more productive activities from the West and sending them into locales with cheaper labor. However, this does not mean that labor was not regulated at the new investment destinations. There are many other countries with large impoverished populations willing to accept, as a start, working long hours for low wages. But labor first had to be organized and disciplined in order to be put to work. The ambitions and

---

[2] Randall Collins, *Macro-History: Essays in Sociology of the Long Run.* (Stanford): Stanford University Press, 1999, CA.

greed of local elites had to be organized and disciplined as well. This is where the coherence of formal state institutions and less formal infrastructural capacities to regulate the social realm through accepted practices and networks could make a crucial difference. Corruption scandals reveal a central element in corporatist state compacts. The kickbacks from businesses in such states form a major part of officials' remuneration. Yet, as the old-time New York politician George Washington Plunkett famously put it, there is "honest graft, and there is dishonest graft." State capacity in this case largely turns on its ability to select officials on the merits of performance, including loyalty to the hierarchy and paternalistic sharing via "honest" graft. This provides a predictable sort of institutional environment that capitalists find attractive.

The cultural and economic legacies of East Asian history, however peculiar they might be, are not entirely unique in their kind. As the global flows of capital continue shifting in the search for new production locales, we can expect more miraculous economic renaissances. India and Turkey already remind us that the past economic geography of Asia was never limited to China. A whole different sector of possibilities seems now emerging from the leftist turn in Latin America where Brazil is laying the tracks. Whatever the ideological rhetoric and tactics of the civic, socialist, nationalist, or indigenous popular movements, in effect they are disestablishing the traditional Latin American politics of oligarchic and military factionalism predicated on foreign dependence. The highly contentious and uneven process spanning the whole continent is now forging, for all its contradictions, genuinely national states. When the leaders of social movements reach state power, they can prevail only by curbing the local powers of provincial notables along with their paramilitary forces, including the drug cartels. One way of doing this is through the imposition of democratic civilian supervision over the armies and police. Another and related way for the consolidation of new democracies is through integrating their citizenry in the centrally sponsored institutions providing for the defense of human rights, social welfare, land tenure, and jobs. Perhaps this is not socialism. It is rather a new and decidedly better variety of capitalism. In the twenty-first century Latin America could at last catch up with social democratic and corporatist state transformations resembling earlier Western patterns, thus also laying foundations for a new wave of industrial development.

A lasting recession in the West, Japan, and the former Soviet bloc, unless things get truly disastrous, might yet boost the industrial ascendance of the former Third World zone. In the past the peripheral and semiperipheral countries often benefited from turmoil in the core because such crisis helped to lower the costs of importing advanced technologies, loosened political controls over world markets, and opened profitable niches to producers with lower labor costs. It is not incidental that the earlier wave of the import-substitution industrializations along the perimeter of the European continent and in Latin America took off in the 1930s–1940s; the export-oriented industrialization of East Asia after the 1970s was fed by outsourcing from the deindustrializing core, and the export markets and drain of resources from the former Soviet republics ought to play a role in the economic expansion of China and especially Turkey.

All five of us consider the narrowing of global inequality gaps a desirable and realistic prospect. In Wallerstein's words, this would minimize pain in the shorter run and maximize the potential for a better world transformation in the medium to longer run. Michael Mann finds here a major source of continued market vitality or even the foundations for a more egalitarian and prosperous world capitalist order modeled on the post-1945 social democratic recovery in Europe. This looks like a good prospect, but can it be compatible with the political economy of capitalism as measured by the rationale of private profit? Neither Wallerstein nor Collins considers the "rise of the rest" as contradicting their hypotheses regarding the future demise of capitalism. To the contrary, the proliferation of new capitalist players in the world markets or the mobile and globally competing educated middle classes would aggravate the dilemmas of capitalism.

So far we remain in the mode of extrapolating the near-past into the near-future. What about major structural shifts, either within high-tech capitalism, in the global world-system, or in the ecology of the planet?

SYSTEMIC LIMITS *VERSUS* ENDLESS INTENSIFICATION

Michael Mann advances an optimistic view of the survival of capitalism, but a rather pessimistic view of environmental crisis. The "rise of the rest" opens virtually limitless new frontiers for capitalism, at least in the foreseeable future. World demographics, and therefore much of the world politics and economy now profoundly affected by the massive growth in the poorer countries and the resulting global migrations into towns, will eventually stabilize. Mann is skeptical of the existence of pansystemic structures and cycles. Instead, he suggests a kaleidoscopic recombination of the four non-congruent and distinctly shaped networks of social power: ideological, economic, military, and political. Leaving his prognosis underdetermined as a matter of principle, Mann refrains from making specific predictions except that capitalism will continue to be resilient, especially if it is steered by more pragmatic liberal-labor politics.

Nevertheless, Mann theorizes from a structured viewpoint elaborating on Max Weber. Wielding his four-dimensional template of power, Mann shows that events become turning points when leading power sources intersect. In the early twentieth century it was the combination of world war with capitalist crisis exacerbated by ideology and politics. In the twenty-first century the combination of rampant capitalist growth with the stalemate of pluralist politics and national self-centeredness points toward ecological crisis. Degrees of contingency exist, but within the structural tendencies laid down by historical development of the four sources of power. It is chiefly because there are multiple causes that unpredictable intersections occur. Here Mann disagrees with Collins and Wallerstein on the importance of crisis in the economic institutions of capitalism. Instead he emphasizes that environmental strains will rise to catastrophe, unless political mobilization prevails to do something about it. Thus Mann's big contingency is in the intersection of the environmental (economic in the largest sense) and the political spheres.

Craig Calhoun agrees with Mann about the centrality of external, especially environmental threats to capitalism. Like all of us, Calhoun argues that the future is not fully determined and therefore it is open to political action. He argues, though, both that internal system risks are more challenging to capitalism than Mann suggests, and that for capitalism to survive there must be a renewal of social institutions that on the one hand enable and facilitate capitalism and on the other hand compensate for the costs and damages it now externalizes as burdens for society at large. The question then is, in the thinking of Wallerstein and Collins, whether such globally escalating costs could be at all sustained by capitalism. The question is not rhetorical. Social scientists should be watching and measuring the dynamic capacities of capitalism to see whether the costs are being met by the generation of new wealth along with the growth or decline in political mechanisms for spreading benefits across the globally connected social structures.

Mann and Calhoun both suggest that a deep environmental crisis could come soon and challenge a still economically viable capitalism. Collins and

Wallerstein see the environmental risk as longer term and capitalist crisis more imminent. Collins reads the scientific consensus of environmental projections as pointing to major crisis around the year 2100. Mann argues that severe ecological damage will threaten some countries' survival already by 2030–50. Yet Collins and Wallerstein project full-scale capitalist crisis in the decades around 2040. They thus suggest that we will confront capitalist crisis before environmental limits become terminal. If one holds the Collins/Wallerstein view, it is tempting to speculate that a socialist resolution to a capitalist crisis would change political structures to such a degree that the ecological crisis could be reasonably handled, as it might well not be if capitalism continues as usual. Mann has a different take on this. Any major capitalist crisis would considerably lower GDP levels, thus easing the environmental crisis (provided warming had not already gone too far). He sees three villains producing climate change: not just capitalism, but also the nation-state and the ordinary mass-consuming citizen. A solution to the crisis would involve reining in and reforming all three. Whether capitalism or socialism (or anything else) emerges viably from the crisis, they would have to be in radically new forms.

Second, both Mann and Calhoun place more emphasis on capitalist dynamism outside the West. Indeed, for Mann, it is not the end of capitalism, but rather the ecological crisis that is global. Hence it cannot be argued that while capitalism and geopolitical hegemony will decline for the United States and Europe, world leadership will pass to other triumphant regions of the globe such as East Asia or a coalition now going under names like the BRICS. However, environmental scientists hold at present that the worst environmental catastrophes will begin in China, South Asia, and Africa. This projection questions the prospect for emergent global leadership providing an alternative to the West. The ecological crisis, according to Mann, could be the end of everybody. Less rhetorically, we have to consider not two alternatives but three: terminal crisis of capitalism as a world-system; decline of the older capitalist hegemons and their replacement by new ones; and global-scale ecological shock, with resulting transformations yet to be envisioned. Collins and Wallerstein argue for the first of these; Mann for the third.

Immanuel Wallerstein and Randall Collins read the picture in different yet mutually compatible ways. They see capitalism as a global system or, if you wish, a hierarchical ecology of economic food chains and market niches. Like any complex system, it has its interrelated structures, dynamic trends, and therefore it must have its ultimate limits. Even if the systemic limits could be expanded thanks to new geographies and technologies of production, they cannot be altogether abolished. Nobody can now specify the institutions and parameters of the world coming after capitalism. Here Craig Calhoun interjects by reminding us how much in such world transitions depends on the contested political choices. Nevertheless Collins and Wallerstein insist that capitalism is nearing its limits, and they make one big prediction: there will be a world transition. They both clearly specify what structural processes are pushing toward the predicted transition, thus opening their hypotheses to critical scrutiny and the possibility of empirical testing. Georgi Derluguian presents the Soviet example as a theoretical and empirical test of what has worked or did not work in the past predictions of Collins and Wallerstein. The trajectory of the Soviet bloc shows how a large systemic unit reaches the limits of its own success and perishes from a combination of structural weights and purely contingent factors.

The differences between the predictions (or future-approximations) of Mann on one hand and those of Collins and Wallerstein on the other correspond to the two sides of the dynamic model of human societies developed by evolutionary anthropologists. In technical terms, it is the "bearing capacity" of a human ecology versus its "productive intensification." According to this model, all hitherto existent human societies tended eventually to fill their environments to saturation, or their bearing capacity. Such limiting crises left three dramatically different possibilities. The first was simply death. A recurrent catastrophe over the entire span of history has been a partial or even total extermination of human groups through famines, epidemics, and genocidal warfare. It is the tragic cycle of Malthusian demographic adjustments in the numbers of humans to be fed. The phases of declining population created conditions for resuming the productive activities on an unchanged basis until the environment was once again filled to bearing capacity, thus provoking another phase of hard times. The second possibility is diversification. It led our ancestors to the discovery and adaptive colonization of new geographic frontiers in the northern tundra and tropical islands, in the steppes, deserts, mountains, and forests—until the human race filled up the planet. Finally, the third possibility is what is usually called progress (i.e., qualitative intensification in the entire technological toolkit), enabling humans to gain ever more from their resources. The latter escape has been the main driving force of evolutionary innovation in human societies.

The complex class societies and first states rose in the productive locales that were too good to abandon, such as the fertile river valleys flanked by the deserts and mountains. The celebrated expression "caging effect" was in fact invented by Michael Mann in his earlier study of ancient empires, markets, and religions.[3] It means that moving away became impossible. Historically, such situations forced some human groups into the qualitatively new, more extensive and elaborate forms of social organization (i.e., new civilizations) that could increase the extraction and exchange of surpluses from the long-occupied locales. The verb "forced into" is intended to stress that many humans would rather not have become slaves, serf peasants, and tribute payers—but they were "caged" by the lack of escape and active coercion from the warrior and priestly elites. In the past, the intensification of productive techniques never came alone but in conjunction with major political and ideological reorganization. These transformative processes were always fraught with considerable conflicts.

In the present book, Michael Mann takes the position that capitalism remains resilient. Once again, Calhoun mostly agrees, though with greater stress on the ways capitalism must change to renew itself. Calhoun also stresses the difference between capitalism in general and the disproportionately financial capitalism that has lately exacerbated systemic risks. Capitalism, according to Mann, has virtually inexhaustible capacities for self-intensification through productive innovations as well as the globalization and deepening of consumer markets. If anything can ever finish capitalism, it will be an outbreak of warfare reaching its destructive limits in the nuclear age, or the planetary crisis of the natural environment. The former operates through causal chains largely independent of the dynamics of capitalism, and thus is contingent (i.e., unpredictable from the standpoint of an internal analysis of capitalism). In the main, this is what separates the positions of Mann and Calhoun from the projections advanced by Wallerstein and Collins. Environmental crisis, however, is one consequence of

---

[3] Michael Mann, *The Sources of Social Power*. Vol. I: *A History of Power from the Beginning to A.D. 1760*. New York: (Cambridge University Press, 1986). Also see the synthesizing essay of Randall Collins "Market Dynamics as the Engine of Historical Change," *Sociological Theory* 8 (1990): 111–35.

capitalist development, intersecting with political and cultural factors. Thus in a roundabout way, capitalism may generate its own downfall, even if, by virtue of intersecting causalities, it doesn't have to be that way.

Randall Collins and Immanuel Wallerstein argue that capitalism is nearing its structural limits. Both acknowledge the extraordinary capacity of capitalism to expand and intensify its own political economy. Capitalism has created the first true world-system encompassing the entire planet with all its populations and productive resources. The displacement of agricultural and industrial jobs by machinery during the nineteenth century did not result in pauperization and revolution in the West, as predicted by Karl Marx in his age, because the development of modern managerial, professional and clerical occupations within private and government bureaucracies created a comfortable cushion of modern middle classes. Nevertheless, in the twenty-first century these spatial and internal reserves will finally be exhausted. If the model focusing on the effects of oligarchic overaccumulation and the distress of the middle classes has relevance across different historical epochs, the terminal crisis of capitalism would actually be a succession of various crises within a protracted period of decline.

Ultimately, however, we all agree that Michael Mann forces us to consider three imponderables: climate change, pandemics, and nuclear warfare. They are not imponderables in the dangers they pose for all of humanity. They are imponderables in terms of the timing of disasters. Our knowledge about each of these is extensive but there are enough uncertainties and differences of views among those who have studied these issues that we cannot be sure what exactly will happen. Climate change seems an unquestionable reality, except for those who reject this reality for political or ideological reasons. Furthermore, everything that has been causing climate change is actually accelerating rather than slowing down. The political differences between wealthier and poorer states as to what should be done about climate change make an accord that would mitigate the risks appear unattainable, at least for now.

However, the earth's ecological complexity is so great, and these changes so extensive, that we do not know what kinds of readjustments will occur. It seems clear that water levels will rise and are already rising, and that this threatens the drowning of vast land areas. It also seems clear that the average temperatures in various parts of the world will change and are already changing. But this can result in shifting the location of agricultural production and energy sources to different zones in ways that might compensate for the acute damage to other zones.

The same thing seems to be true of pandemics. The enormous advances of world medicine in the last hundred or so years that have seemed to bring so many diseases under control have simultaneously created a situation in which humanity's ancient enemy, the germ, has had to find new ways to be resistant. Once again, our knowledge seemed great but, when all is said and done, it turns out to be pitifully small. In this race against time, how fast will we learn? And how much must we unlearn in order to survive?

There remains the specter of extermination from nuclear weapons. Ever since the end of the Cold War and the hubristic attempt to impose an American unipolarity, nuclear proliferation has become virtually unavoidable. There might not be imminent danger in terms of interstate warfare. Indeed it is almost the contrary. Nuclear weapons are essentially defensive weapons and therefore reduce, not increase, the likelihood of interstate wars. Nevertheless, there remain several imponderables. The motivations of nonstate actors are not necessarily the same as those of responsible officials. No doubt there are some who would like to get their hands on nuclear weapons (as well as on chemical and biological weapons) and use them. The limited ability of many states to protect such weapons from seizure or purchase may facilitate their acquisition by nonstate actors. And the possibility of a rogue state agent, the Dr. Strangelove of fiction, is never to be ruled out.

It is quite possible that the world will weather the global transition without any of these catastrophes occurring. But it is also possible that it will not. A lot will depend on what will be the new political structures and how soon they can emerge. Conceivably such new structures will take the kinds of measures that can reduce, even eliminate, the likelihood of global disasters. Let us be clear, these are not just natural disasters. Famine, pestilence, nuclear terrorism are decidedly political challenges to humanity. That is why we call them imponderables. The search for effective countermeasures means making political choices. One major way in which many people react to these dangers is to pull inward in a heavily protectionist and xenophobic way. We see this tendency already almost everywhere. It means that those who seek a system that is relatively democratic and relatively egalitarian have to work harder at developing political strategies that will counter this trend.

TRANSITIONS

One big thing we all agree on is that in coming decades the familiar configurations of global political economy are bound to change in significant and not immediately evident ways. Politicians, social movements, and media commentators will be at a loss trying to steer through the coming years on the old conventional wisdom. Governments and once dominant business corporations are going to find their levers of power weakened, their well-practiced moves in the political and ideological repertoires useless or presenting ever new problems down the road. The protesters might feel as outraged as ever. But they will be much less sure against whom to protest, what to demand, how to organize, and with whom to ally themselves. Our theoretical knowledge of the past historical transitions will prove only an imperfect adviser. In the years ahead our theories will require considerable corrections and additions. (But isn't this the nature of scientific knowledge?) In part, this is because many problems and prospects appear unprecedented in human history. In the main, however, we know that major historical transitions occur simultaneously at several different levels. Business as usual becomes impossible in times of transition. American imperial hegemony is visibly faltering, as geopolitical theory has long predicted. Its biggest reserves in the productivity, finances, and political compliance of China and the European Union are running out. A big question is how precipitous or gradual will be the coming decline of the West. Our best hope perhaps is a negotiated (i.e., nondestructive) equalization in the shares of power and wealth between the historical West and the rising rest of the world.

The key point of agreement, to stress it again, is that the future is not preordained in any great detail. Open-ended political struggles will play a crucial role in selecting the routes and collective destinations. Moreover, social science can make a difference in the coming years. Macrohistorical theories warn against disastrous future possibilities. A middle-ground possibility is fragmentation and involution (i.e., continuing along essentially the same lines only in a lessened, crippled, and worse off shape). Here the recent fate of the Soviet Union serves as the nearest example. Still another nasty possibility is a fascist-like dictatorship supported by social movements of aggrieved nationals and reliant on a militaristic and highly invasive police state. Unfortunately, the record of twentieth-century fascism shows that it could produce, at least for a few decades, viable political economies where large groups of people benefit from oppressing other large groups of people. The exceptionally vicious and megalomaniac Nazi regime in Germany perished from the external war, not from internal political transformation or revolution.

Yet the same theories point to a strong possibility of more hopeful pathways through the chaotic years ahead of us. Our hopes derive from the theoretically grounded observation that human responses to the big structural crises in the past tended to build up qualitatively new and more extensive collective powers. This trend developed through periodic collapses and bursts of human inventiveness (though far from always peaceful) that would eventually pave the way for new periods of stabilization and prosperity.

The human race is now facing another such sequence, and this time it is the entire humanity populating the planet. Our late friend and colleague Giovanni Arrighi used to say that systemic problems call for systemic solutions. In his analytical model, the trajectory of historical capitalism went through several cresting waves of spatial expansions and restructurings.[4] European capitalists had originally secured themselves and their enterprise by acquiring their own national states—with the armies, navies, and the taxation machinery that support them—amid the formative chaos of the sixteenth century. In more analytical terms, capitalism obtained its historical breakthrough in the internalization of protection costs. The next wave brought the deepening of capitalism and its tremendous colonial expansion based on the internalization of production costs, or what is commonly known as the British-led industrial revolution of the 1780s–1840s. But that epoch also ushered in multiple crises flowing from the effects of the business cycle, the institutionalization of revolutionary and reform movements, and the competitive geopolitics of industrial imperialism that in 1914 nearly killed capitalism. The American hegemony of the twentieth century helped to tame these crises by adding another layer of complexity: the internalization of transaction costs. The acute need to stabilize the capitalist system against multiple dangers is what after 1945 determined the elaborate and imposing architecture of modern governments, economic corporations, and international organizations.

---

[4] Giovanni Arrighi, *The Long Twentieth Century: Money, Power and the Origins of Our Times.* (Updated edition). (London: Verso, 2010).

Logically then, the epochal accomplishment remaining for the twenty-first century is the internalization of the costs of social and environmental reproduction to be achieved at a truly planetary level. Consider a fact that seems too big to enter the usual policy debates. During the last ten thousand years or so the majority of humankind lived in villages. The invention (rather, the repeated inventions) of village community marked a major reorganization in collective human capabilities. It made possible what archeologists call the Neolithic revolution, and thus agrarian societies. The pattern of village life permitted midsized groups of nonrelatives to organize their common affairs in a robust and comprehensive manner. It took care of everything that mattered for social reproduction: division of labor, the traditional regulation of resources, daily life tensions and conflicts, the transmission of culture and skills, the ideological (or even cosmological) rituals of group solidarity, from the highly mystical to the mundane village dance. In sum, village community organized the functional and emotional aspects of the human life cycle from birth to death. And self-organizing villages served as tributary bases for all the subsequent complex societies, from tribal chiefdoms to city-states and empires.

Capitalism originally emerged into what was still a world of villages. The market and geopolitical dynamism of capitalism soon began undermining village communities because the villagers were needed elsewhere as labor, colonists, and soldiers. On their side, the villagers themselves often found it impossible to stay in their poor and constraining rural locales. The causes of village extinction go by many different names such as modernization, urbanization, industrialization, agrarian overpopulation, the spread of literacy, or imperialism and military revolution. The net effect eventually would be the same everywhere—first in the West, next in Japan, the Soviet bloc, and now all over—draining the countryside of its once numerous inhabitants and moving them into the cities or, even more commonly, into the slums.

The transition from village to town as the main organizing locus of human life appears irreversible. Its implications help explain why the crisis of capitalism is so hard to solve. Something must step in to resume the comprehensive provision of normative order, social regulation, daily security and welfare in the new agglomerations of humanity. Moreover, these tasks must be now performed not only on a vastly larger scale but also better than the villages used to do. Lest we forget, villages provided intimate coziness and shelter that meant, by extension, intrusive supervision and the social caging

186 • DOES CAPITALISM HAVE A FUTURE?

of individuals. The protective inertia of traditions, the inequalities of age and sex inscribed in the patriarchal households, the denigrating and violently vengeful attitudes toward strangers and outsiders were part and parcel of village life, too.

The modern history of mass migrations, demographic transitions, and the creation of new political communities brought enormous costs and traumas. The overseas emigration of European settlers helped to improve the ratio of demographics to resources at the cost of the displacement, enslavement, and downright extermination of the indigenous peoples in the colonies who lacked guns and immunity to the germs brought by the invaders. The emergence of modern nations often implied the oppression and expulsion of the "non-national" minorities. After 1914 the radical mutation of nationalism into militarist and virulently populist strains of fascism escalated the same historical vectors into the Holocaust. In a different kind of radical escalation, the Soviet collectivization of agriculture sacrificed human lives by the millions for the sake of achieving industrialization and modern life for the children of survivors. Only after 1945 were the former peasants and working classes of the West and Soviet bloc factored into social security and prosperity by their national states. In total, this amounted to several hundred millions of people. But are there now the resources, let alone political will, to factor in several billion people from the global South?

Enthusiasts of globalization hail our moving into a global village. This sanguine claim should be evaluated soberly. Cosmopolitanism is a long-standing project that has had its liberal and socialist versions.[5] But it means something different as a complement to a world of stable states. And there exist other, more conservative projects for directing globalization that derive their energies from imperialist ambitions, nationalisms, anti-immigrant rejections, religious fundamentalism, and their combinations. The very possibility of an arena of global governance and a common human identity may well become the main focus of political contention in the coming decades. The outcome is too early to predict. Systemic crisis at a world scale will sow havoc, panic, and nasty reactions. But it will also elicit collective coping strategies going in the direction of a more democratically accountable, organizationally flexible, and capable global governance. Humanity can still

[5] More in Craig Calhoun, *Nations Matter: Culture, History and the Cosmopolitan Dream*. New York: Routledge, 2007.

escape a catastrophic backslide in the complexity and extent of its collective organization. Perhaps enough lessons of twentieth-century revolutionary and socially reformist movements have withstood the neoconservative ravages of recent decades. Or it could be something profoundly changing in the complex and contradictory institutional architecture of the modern states themselves. At the very least, here is yet another topic for fruitful investigation by social scientists.

We are reluctant to call the "state," let alone "global state," the political structure of a better future. This is in fact the biggest unknown. Let us make just a couple of observations regarding the pattern of politics in a more hopeful future. Most of us doubt that existing international organizations add up to the prototype of such structures. The United Nations, the European Union, the IMF, Davos, G-8, G-20 and other such clubs belong to the epoch of capitalist integration and American hegemony. At present these institutions are weakened or compromised by political manipulation and technocratic aloofness. Some of us, however, see the only solution to environmental crisis in a much stronger network of relations between states— a Super United Nations. Others of us doubt that this political integration can be achieved fast enough, and it is not without its own worries. Still, the post-1945 epoch of relative world peace and prosperity set an important precedent that may prove more lasting than its political institutions.

The changing structures and directions of future politics will surely deliver big surprises. The majority of people regard extension of prior experience as most plausible. The inexorable growth of national states has been indeed a major reality during the entire modern period. But what if the novel recombination of seemingly familiar factors at a planetary level turns out differently? After all, this is exactly what Randall Collins argues regarding the newest technological displacement. Although none of us considers anarchism a very realistic strategy, we must admit that the antiestablishment spirit of 1968 proved one of its most enduring legacies, both on the left and on the right. Perhaps this calls for taking more seriously the values and organizational alternatives represented by the nonstatist movements tenaciously surviving in the margins. The major transformative mobilizations of state powers and peoples in modern times have been associated with wars and violent revolutions. Anarchist or libertarian calls could not be politically effective in such situations. But what if the future delivers a major nonmilitary emergency, be it frightening extinctions of biological species or middle-class jobs? Let us seriously consider what makes us believe that states or interstate alliances will prove up to the task of organizing billions of people for the altruistic enterprise of planting trees and developing new technologies or educating the children, caring for the elderly, and overall sustaining life? A self-organizing dynamic might become rather the order of the day. Who knows? This might even open common grounds for bridging the hostility between the popular movements now raging on the right and left. Here we may identify another moving front of social science inquiry into the dynamics of contemporary ideology and popular politics.

SOCIAL SCIENCE IN A TRANSFORMATIVE FUTURE

Are political hopes blurring our theoretical visions? Our answer is this: Reflexively admitting a connection between our hopes and our hypotheses is a necessary component of theoretical honesty in social science, especially when dealing with our own times. Social theory is often likened to lenses of various cuts that enable us to discern patterns in human action. When the lenses are cut solely to confirm one's faith and denounce whatever opposes it, the resulting vision is strictly ideological. Such lenses, commonly worn in politics and public debating, function more like blinders. Theory is different because it has to be testable. What constitutes tests in social science has been a matter of controversy. We are methodological pluralists insofar as we doubt attempts to legislate the one right way of doing social science. Yet we are not complete relativists. Different kinds of problems and scales of analysis leave researchers the choice of investigative techniques. Experiments and statistical correlations have an important place in the toolkit of social science but their role cannot be universal. Disciplined ethnographic observation is often more revealing in studying localized social environments. At the macrohistorical level, which is where we work, the main method might be likened to connecting the dots in a big puzzle. Another test for macrohistorical theory are counterfactuals, the alternative roads that seemed possible at one historical juncture but were not taken. In other words, we must show both how we get from one historical situation to another and what are the actual range of structural possibilities and the factors on which events turn. This is perhaps as close we can get to an experiment in our kind of research.

Historical social science from the outset has dealt with conflict, transitions, and mutations. Hence the main question of this book: What if the future is fraught with major crises? Social landscapes are fluid and often turbulent, perhaps more like weather maps. Local events are inherently contingent even if in retrospect we can explain them by pinpointing which structures had shifted or broken down, and what human action, emerging from specific positions, ended up taking the emergent opportunities. Predicting events in the longer run is futile, but predicting structural configurations is not. Take the weather analogy. It would be irresponsible to predict that next year, say, on the 13th of January it will snow in Chicago. This is the "short" time of contingent events. But it would seem trivial to predict that it will snow in Chicago next January. This statement belongs to the longer-run time of structures. However, what about several decades into the future when Chicago climate might come to resemble hurricane-prone Florida or, alternatively, frozen Siberian tundra?

Readers seeking exact future scenarios in this book may feel frustrated. Their frustration is unwarranted. Lack of precision in social forecasting means that collectively we face a certain freedom of action on a spate of structurally available options. The options are rather limited in normal times although even then there exists political choice between somewhat better and somewhat worse outcomes. But the options become vastly magnified in periods of crisis when the usual mechanisms of status quo are breaking down. Such times call for a conscious strategy of systemic transformation. Humans do make their futures, in conflict and association with other humans, even if not in the circumstances of their own choosing. Social science should clarify what are the circumstances and emerging possibilities, especially when the possibilities may be opening and closing rapidly.

On this score we are critical of contemporary social science for its willful abstraction from structural possibilities of historical change. Our charges equally apply to two very different mainstream currents—postmodernism and neoclassical economics—that have come to dominate academic social sciences since the 1980s. Both, in their own ways, reflect the nameless period following the crisis decade of the 1970s, the decline of leftist movements, and the relaunching of American hegemonic ambitions in the project of neo-conservative globalization.

Various intellectual currents, stronger in the humanities and summarily grouped under the rubric of postmodernism, became extremely skeptical of any big theories or what they called "master-narratives." Instead they celebrated doubt, irony, lived experience, deconstruction of beliefs, and the minute interpretations of cultural practices. This intellectual movement grew directly from the revolts of 1968 and the demographic shifts in the composition of academia with the advent of women and minorities. The shift of attention to the ways in which humans imagine themselves and envision their social universes helped to instill a new critical awareness of the matters of faith that had hitherto remained unspoken and unexamined. The post-modernist movement stirred many stagnant waters, but it left them muddied.

On the opposite side, the field of social science fell under the domination of neoclassical economics and its formalistic emulators in other disciplines. The structures underpinning this situation are not too different from the erstwhile influence of astrology. A healthy dose of Swiftean parody may be in order here. Astrology before modern times, like economics today, was established expertise. It enjoyed the ears of the rulers in virtually all civilizations, East and West. It brought generous remuneration because the highest remuneration is commanded by the experts in the areas of highest human uncertainty and anxiety. In the imperial and feudal political structures based on the familial control of rent, the greatest elite anxieties were associated with dynastic succession and rapidly turning luck in warfare. In much the same way, capitalist anxieties derive from uncertain investment choices, market volatility, and the popular opposition that their operations occasionally generate. Astrology, like neoclassical economics, both functioned as ideological disciplines conforming to the common sense of the contemporary dominant classes. Astrology at its heyday, however, was more than merely a reflection of elite ideology. At its best, astrology was a highly mathematized discipline based on centuries-long accumulation of empirical observations which became the foundation of modern astronomy. Since things turned out as predicted only about half of the time, practical forecasting was subtly corrected by intuition and political acumen. A successful astrologer had to master the demeanor of an astute courtier. Much the same applies to practicing business advisers and government economists in our day.

In times of crisis and resulting political polarization economists and political scientists will find plenty of opportunities to do something new. There will be whole new fronts of pathbreaking research, for instance, in the alternative organization of markets. The dismissal of market possibilities was a major theoretical and practical mistake of twentieth-century leftist movements. We treat with great respect the intellectual legacy of Joseph Schumpeter. But what will be the future uses of his theory of entrepreneurial dynamism? Who or what could play the role of entrepreneurs in the future, even beyond the crisis of capitalism? Is it possible to harness entrepreneurial energies toward more market creativity and less destruction?

No less seriously we take Karl Polanyi's idea of 'fictitious commodities', like land, money, and human life, that cannot be traded. In the twenty-first century "land" broadly means the environment, "money" is global finance, and "human life" stands for the internationalization of the costs of social reproduction through the public support of decent and affordable health-care, education, housing, pensions, and not least, physical security of our cities. Can a postcapitalist world economy be structured into sectors operating on different principles: the priority of social reproduction in the sector of broadly construed public utilities and the priority of market effectiveness in the sector of consumer goods and services? Moreover, the postcapitalist economic systems may themselves not be static. Periodic reversion to market economies with private property, in some degree or another, may well occur in the future. The world may see yet more swings between capitalist and noncapitalist arrangements of the economy. This too will have to be managed.

No less politically harmful than the aversion to markets is the aversion to the directing power of states. Far from coincidentally, the neoconservative restoration during the last decades of the twentieth century in the wake of collapses on the political left, relentlessly challenged state powers through deregulation and globalization. Capitalists grew suspicious of "Big Government" for the quite real reason that modern states potentially could be captured by the non-elite citizens—in democratic elections, street insurrections, or both—and used for the noncapitalist purposes of market regulation and social redistribution. Big welfare state had to be tolerated, to a degree, immediately after 1945 for the sake of resumed peace. But by the 1970s many capitalists, especially in America, had become emboldened by the opportunity to defeat the left and roll back postwar compromises. Now a major question for theorizing is whether the modern bureaucratic state can play a good role, bad role, or no role at all in steering our collective affairs through times of crisis and the looming systemic transformation. This big question falls into many subordinate questions, practical issues, and theoretical paradoxes that remain to be explored. Social scientists will have plenty of intellectual work of crucial importance in rising to these challenges.

CODA

This quintet of authors gathered to sketch the range of destinations where the world may be headed. We have summarized and refocused on the future many arguments from our previously written volumes. Intentionally, this is not a single-tune quintet. The hope was to achieve counterpoint and provoke each other into pursuing the implications of our individual themes. We have included the complexities, caveats, and dissents. We have not avoided the dramatic, even thunderous notes. Such tonalities seemed warranted by the enormity and gravity of the main themes. The coming decades will be anything but usual: that is, usual in the perspective of the last 500 years. The collective trajectory of humanity is taking a big turn, but not necessarily for the worse.

A rising note of optimism emerges in the finale. A big crisis and transformation, whatever its scenario, does not mean the world is coming to an end. There is no reason to believe, on the basis of the accumulated understandings of sociology, that history will ever end, as long as there are human beings connected in social organization. The direst scenarios involving a world nuclear war or environmental collapse, fortunately, seem avoidable precisely because collective extinction has been widely regarded as a real danger for some decades now. The end of capitalism is not a catastrophe of that sort. A crisis in the bearing structures of the modern world's political economy is far from a doomsday prediction. Ultimately, the end of capitalism is a hopeful vision. Yes, it comes with its own dangers. We must remember how early twentieth-century attempts to foster anticapitalist alternatives in response to crisis developed totalitarian tendencies and ended in bureaucratic inertia. Nor should we forget how directly these anticapitalist projects arose from the state machineries and personnel constructed in the world wars. The crucial political vectors in the coming decades will have to be curbing militarism and institutionalizing democratic human rights around the planet. An impasse in the political economy of capitalism brings us to historical junctures where what has been long regarded utopian may yet acquire technically feasible foundations in a new kind of political economy. It may yet help us to deal better with threats to our planet's biosphere, and many other tasks that humanity will be facing later in this century.

Those who worry about postcapitalism ushering in a period of deadly stagnation are surely wrong. Those who hope that postcapitalism will deliver a lasting paradise without its own crises are likely wrong, too. After the crisis—and, some of us predict, the postcapitalist transition of the mid-21st century—there will be a great deal happening. Hopefully, much of it will be good. We shall see, and soon enough.